COPING WITH THE CULTS

Lorri MacGregor

COPING WITH THE CULTS

Copyright © 1992 by Harvest House Publishers
Eugene, Oregon 97402

Library of Congress Cataloging-in-Publication Data

MacGregor, Lorri, 1942-
    Coping with the cults / Lorri MacGregor.
    ISBN 0-89081-940-8
    1. Cults—Controversial literature.   2. Sects—Controversial litera-
ture.   I. Title.
BP603.M25   1992   91-37787
291.9—dc20   CIP

Printed in the United States of America.

CONTENTS

Introduction

INTRODUCTION

This book was written as a manual for quick reference on the cults from a Christian perspective. It is intended to be easily understood by the "ordinary" Christian. We feel that we have hit the main points of doctrine in each of the various cults discussed and have eliminated for the reader much of the tediousness and long quotations found in other publications on the same subject.

Our primary purpose in writing this book is to equip Christians to witness effectively to cult members and win them for Christ. Before this can be done, it is necessary to have some basic understanding of the cults.

On a personal note, Lorri MacGregor was for 15 years a Jehovah's Witness. In all that time, only one Christian took the time to seriously "contend for the faith" with her and finally win her for Christ. That Christian was Keith MacGregor, who later became her husband. Their burden was for those still trapped in the cults. God called them into full-time ministry in 1979. Since that time God has blessed them with many souls set free from the cults. Their outreach has now spread worldwide.

MacGregor Ministries is a registered nonprofit society in Canada and is active in teaching seminars, radio and television outreaches, video and film projects, and personal ministry. *Coping with the Cults* has enjoyed wide acceptance among Christians with a heart for reaching the cults.

COPING
WITH THE
CULTS

Chapter 1

HOW TO IDENTIFY
A CULT

The subject of cults often causes confusion. *Webster's Dictionary* defines a cult as: 1. a system of religious worship; 2. devoted attachment to a person, principle, etc.; 3. a sect. *Webster's* then goes on to define a sect as a "religious denomination."

With this hazy definition for a cult, it is no wonder people are confused. We need to turn from the pages of the dictionary to the pages of the Bible.

A Cult Is Counterfeit Christianity

"Counterfeit Christianity"—an imitation of real Christianity—is probably the best description we can give for a cult. Bible terms such as "Jesus Christ," "resurrection," "salvation," and "atonement" are used by cults, but entirely different meanings have been assigned to these terms by the various cult groups.

Like counterfeit money which is sometimes difficult to detect, so it is difficult to detect counterfeit Christianity since it looks like the real thing. Experts examining counterfeit money often hold it up to a strong light and look for

identifying marks. Counterfeit Christianity also has identifying marks which can be seen when held up to an even
stronger light: the light of God's Word, the Bible.

We are repeatedly warned in Scripture to watch out for
false prophets, false teachers, and false doctrine. To do
this, we need to examine the prophecies, teachings, and
doctrines of the various groups claiming to be Christian,
and then we need to expose them. This is what the apostle
Paul did in 2 Timothy 2:17,18 where he said, "Among them
are Hymenaeus and Philetus, men who have gone astray
from the truth saying that the resurrection has already
taken place, and thus they upset the faith of some." Jesus
named "the deeds of the Nicolaitans, which I also hate"
(Revelation 2:6).

All this "detecting" of a cult takes time, so we need some
methods whereby we can readily detect a cult without
time-consuming research. This is possible, and we outline
the methods here.

Early Detection and the True Church

We are at an advantage if we know what to expect from a
cult. Cultists are very well-trained to appear "Christian,"
and indeed believe that they are the true church and you
need the deliverance!

Therefore be bold and ask the question, "Do you believe
the group you represent is the *only true church* on the face
of the earth?" If they reply that they are or if they are
evasive, making remarks like, "Well, every church has a
measure of truth *but* . . ." you have made an early detection
of a cult.

Every Christian if asked the same question, regardless
of his denomination, would reply that the true church is
comprised of believers in the Lord Jesus Christ, and that

He (not some organization) is *the way, the truth, and the life* (John 14:6). No legitimate denomination would claim that it and its members alone have salvation *exclusively*, but the cults (the counterfeits) do.

Early Detection and the Bible

Again under the subject of early detection of a cult, find out if the person talking to you believes in *more than the Bible*.

For example, the Mormons will *say* they believe the Bible, but they will be anxious to let you know that they have *further revelation* in the form of the *Book of Mormon, Doctrine and Covenants,* and *Pearl of Great Price,* which they also consider inspired.

Jehovah's Witnesses believe the Bible (especially their own altered version, *The New World Translation,* which has altered most Scriptures dealing with the deity of Christ). Jehovah's Witnesses will tell you that the Bible can only be understood by their particular organization, the Watch Tower Society. I often ask Jehovah's Witnesses, "Has anyone ever become a Jehovah's Witness by studying the Bible alone?" Of course not. Other cults also believe they have *exclusive understanding* of the Bible as it is explained to them by their particular prophet.

Watch out for those trying to interpret Scripture for you who use the Bible like a dictionary. That is, they make their point and then refer to isolated texts, often hopscotching all over the Bible to "prove" their point. Used this way, the Bible can be made to say almost anything.

Also, be careful of groups stressing prophecy out of proportion to other subjects in Scripture. "Prophecy seminars" are often the first step into a cult group.

Remember also that it is the Holy Spirit who will guide you into all truth, not some self-appointed prophet or organization. John 16:13 reads, "But when He, the Spirit of truth comes, He will guide you into all the truth; for He will not speak on His own initiative, but whatever He hears, He will speak; and He will disclose to you what is to come."

Where Are the Cults Evangelizing?

The Holy Spirit through the apostle Paul gives the church divine warning in 2 Corinthians 11:4 that there will be those *coming to us* (that is, the church) and preaching to us "another Jesus," a "different gospel," with a "different spirit." This is perhaps the best definition in the Bible of a cult.

In verses 13 and 14 Paul further tells us that their leaders will be disguised as "apostles of Christ." Although satanically inspired, they will appear as "angel[s] of light." Therefore do not think a cult has to appear bad to be bad. On the contrary, a cult often looks extra-good. How do you think the person at your door became so deceived, except that the cult looked so good to that individual? Bear in mind that you usually are not talking to a deliberate deceiver but to a poor, misguided soul. Cults may look genuinely Christian, perhaps like just another denomination. Do not look on the outward appearance—use your detectors!

Many cults have begun as "interdenominational Bible study groups." Neighborhood study groups are fine as long as they function under the headship outlined in the Bible in Ephesians 4:11-16.

And He gave some as apostles, and some as prophets, and some as evangelists, and some as pastors and teachers, for the equipping of the saints for the work of service, to the building up of the body of Christ; until we all attain to the unity of the faith, and of the knowledge of the Son of God, to a mature man, to the measure of the stature which belongs to the fulness of Christ. As a result, we are no longer to be children, tossed here and there by waves, and carried about by every wind of doctrine, by the trickery of men, by craftiness in deceitful scheming; but speaking the truth in love, we are to grow up in all aspects into Him, who is the head, even Christ from whom the whole body, being fitted and held together by that which every joint supplies, according to the proper working of each individual part, causes the growth of the body for the building up of itself in love.

Watch out for "one-man shows" where the leader does not answer to anyone but himself. The biblical arrangement is one of submission to others to protect the body of Christ. Don't remove yourself from that protection by following one "lone ranger" leader. As long as he is teaching truth you are fine, but if he goes out into "left field" with some doctrine, you will go with him into deception. Stay under the Bible's arrangement for the protection of Christ's body. Don't isolate yourself by committing totally to one person as your "shepherd."

The purpose of the cults is to divide the body of Christ. The thrust of their "missionary activities" is not to the unchurched but to believers in Christ. Missionaries often tell of going to the unsaved and preaching the gospel, finally getting a church going, and then "here come the cults!" We all need to heed the warning in Scripture, "Keep your eye on those who cause dissensions and hindrances... and turn away from them" (Romans 16:17).

Detect What "Salvation" the Cult Offers

Without fail, the cults have done away with salvation by *grace* alone. Their salvation is always *grace plus works*, and in their organizations you can never be *sure* of your salvation until your death or "until Armageddon." Cults keep you in a constant state of anxiety and fear of impending judgment. The strongest witness the Christian can present in this situation is the *assurance* they have *right now* that they are saved. Good works are a result of salvation, not a condition of salvation.

> For by *grace* you have been saved through faith; and that not of yourselves, it is the *gift of God; not as a result of works*, that no one should boast (Ephesians 2:8,9, emphasis added).

> God has *given us* eternal life, and this life is in His Son. These things I have written to you who *believe* in the name of the Son of God, in order that you may *know* that you *have eternal life* (1 John 5:11,13, emphasis added).

Recognize the Two Classes in the Cults

In the world of the cults there are two classes of people. At the high levels we find the *deceivers*. At the lower levels, we find the *deceived*. You will usually be dealing with the honest-hearted *deceived* ones, so remember our instructions in 2 Timothy 2:24-26,

And the Lord's bond-servant must not be quarrelsome, but be kind to all, able to teach, patient when wronged, with gentleness correcting those who are in opposition, if perhaps God may grant them repentance, leading to the knowledge of the truth, and they may come to their senses and escape from the snare of the devil, having been held captive by him to do his will.

Those using 2 John as an excuse not to witness to cultists should realize that this admonition not to let such a one into their house is referring to anyone who "does not abide in the teaching of Christ" (verse 9)—obviously the now-departed members of the Christian congregation. This describes most high-ranking cult leaders, but those at your door usually have never "abided" in the doctrine of Christ. Indeed, most of them have had Christ misrepresented to them and do not even know who Christ really is.

What Do the Cults Think of Jesus Christ?

This question is the most important one we could possibly ask, for every cult presents "another Jesus" (2 Corinthians 11:4). Listed at the end of this book are the names of the various cults and their teachings on the person of Jesus Christ. Cults are often unwilling to share with you their *real* view on Christ until they have drawn you in and won your friendship. It may be necessary for *you* to present *them* with their own doctrine and confront them on this most important issue. Remember, if we have the right Jesus Christ we are right for all eternity, but if we have the wrong Jesus Christ, we are wrong for all eternity.

The prime question to ask the cultist is, "Do you believe that Jesus Christ is *Almighty* God, manifest in the flesh?" (Matthew 1:23; John 1:1,14, etc.). If they cannot agree, you have detected a cult. Jesus is *not* some lesser or extra god, or any kind of an angel. He is not just one of many prophets and gurus, or an extraordinarily good man, but He is *the only true God* (1 Timothy 1:16,17). As Jesus is truly God, He is also truly man (Romans 5:15; 1 Timothy 2:5). This is the Jesus Christ of the Bible: truly God, truly man. For a fuller explanation, please refer to chapter 9.

Cults Often Humanize God and Deify Man

Eastern mysticism and humanism have been making steady inroads of late into the Christian church. Beware of any teacher telling you that you can be "a god" or "part of God" or the "Godhead" or "Godfamily." Especially be on guard for those calling God a "Godforce." Remember the original lie that Satan whispered in Eve's ear way back in the Garden of Eden was that she could be "as God" or "a god." There is only one true God (Deuteronomy 6:4), and we are His creation, not His equal. Watch out for groups that humanize God and deify man.

In Conclusion

Remember that persons who have been led into cults have gone because they were sincerely seeking for God, and no true Christian bore witness to them. Or after receiving Christ they received wrong teaching, supposing that what they did pleased God. Cults are clever counterfeits for those not grounded solidly in Bible teachings. It is not too late to lead them to the true Christ or win them back to their original commitment.

Remember to fight *spiritual battles* with *spiritual weapons*. Prayer is your chief weapon. You will not be able to proceed on your own strength, but remember that Christ provides the strength. Paul wrote in Philippians 4:13, "I can do all things through Him who strengthens me."

Remember, too, the authority you have as a Christian. Jesus promised His followers in Luke 10:19: "Behold, I have given you authority . . . over all the power of the enemy, and nothing shall injure you."

You need not fear witnessing to those in cult groups. Second Timothy 1:7 says, "For God hath not given us the spirit of fear; but of power, and of love, and of a sound mind" (KJV).

Prepare yourself to witness as the Holy Spirit makes opportunity for you by becoming acquainted with cult views on Christ and salvation, as well as the Scriptures to correct these views.

Some have found it helpful to study up on mind-control and deprogramming methods from a secular viewpoint, but we prefer to use spiritual rather than worldly methods. After many years of setting people free from cults, we can testify to the power of the Word of God to set matters straight. Hebrews 4:12 reads,

> For the word of God is living and active and sharper than any two-edged sword, and piercing as far as the division of soul and spirit, of both joints and marrow, and able to judge the thoughts and intentions of the heart.

We have found prayer and the Word of God to be the best combination available when dealing with people in the cults and helping them come to freedom in Christ.

Chapter 2

HOW JEHOVAH'S WITNESSES TWIST THE SCRIPTURES

O f all the cult groups, Jehovah's Witnesses are the ones that are the most deceitful and clever when it comes to the twisting and distorting of the Bible. The ones at your door are not responsible, but are deceived by those at headquarters. I was formerly a Jehovah's Witness for 15 years, and understand that organization from the inside out. Those in control are so clever in their distortions that members are convinced that they are continually receiving "truth." They even inquire, "How long have you been in the truth?" (meaning the Jehovah's Witness organization).

At my very first encounter with Jehovah's Witnesses, they put the twist on John 14:28 where Jesus said, "The Father is greater than I," and told me the Trinity was a doctrine of Satan, Jesus was inferior to His Father, and Jesus was an archangel named Michael. How proficient they seemed flipping all over the Bible from one (unrelated) Scripture to another! I was impressed. As our "Bible studies" progressed, I was warned, "Work out your own salvation with fear and trembling," quoting only a portion of the thought in Philippians 2:12. I was told this consisted of "publishing the good news of God's kingdom" by selling their publications door-to-door, attending five meetings a week, and meeting numerous other quotas. Of course I was never directed to the following verse, which continued the same sentence: "for it is God who is at work in you, both to will and to work for His good pleasure" (Philippians 2:13).

The Jehovah's Witnesses at headquarters want to make sure their members know nothing of the indwelling Christ ("for it is God who is at work *in you*..."), and they have removed this truth from numerous Scriptures in their "bible." Everywhere that it says "Christ *in you*" they have altered the text to read *"in union with you."* However, worse distortions are yet to be discussed.

How Reliable Is the New World Translation?

Many scholars will not even apply the term "translation" to this "bible." The Watch Tower Society needed a bible to conform to their strange doctrines, and so they created one. The "translation" was done by a five-member committee in Brooklyn, New York. Four of these men had a high school education only, with no Hebrew or Greek knowledge at all. The fifth man, Fred W. Franz, although claiming to know Hebrew and Greek (without credentials), while under oath in a Scottish court of law failed a simple Hebrew test. He was a college sophomore dropout and lied about being offered a Rhodes scholarship. No wonder the Watch Tower Society refuses to name the translators who they say prefer to be anonymous and "humble"! No reputable scholar will endorse this "translation," which distorts the truth about the Lord Jesus Christ.

Distorting John 1:1

"In (the) beginning the Word was, and the Word was with God, and the Word was a god" (NWT). Since the Jehovah's Witnesses portray Jesus as a lesser god, the archangel Michael, and merely a man on earth, they needed a bible to suit their misrepresentations. They had to forego legitimate scholarship and translation and finally came up with three sources to agree with them. Let's examine these sources.

1. The New Testament by Johannes Greber. The Watch Tower Society quoted Johannes Greber extensively in their publications (*The Word, Who Is He?* p. 5; *Make Sure of All Things* (1965), p. 489; *Aid to Bible Understanding*, pp. 1134, 1669, etc.). Upon examining this "New Testament" we find that Johannes Greber was a spiritist and also authored a book called *Communication with the Spirit World of God*. He reported seeing the translation come in "large illuminated letters and words passing before his eyes." Other times he reports that his wife, "a medium of God's spirit world," conveyed the correct answers from "God's messengers to Pastor Greber."

As we examine this New Testament further we find constant references to God's holy spirits (plural), and it becomes more and more obvious that we are dealing with a man deep into spiritism. This, of course, is forbidden by God's Word. Leviticus 19:31 says, "Do not turn to mediums or spiritists; do not seek them out to be defiled by them."

Did the Watch Tower Society seek out this spiritist? Yes, for the Johannes Greber Memorial Foundation provided another cult ministry with a photocopy of a letter from the Watch Tower Society acknowledging receipt of not only several of his New Testaments but also Greber's book *Communication with the Spirit World of God.* Why has the Watch Tower Society of Jehovah's Witnesses willingly and knowingly been in communication with a spiritistic society?

It's true that in the April 1, 1983 *Watchtower* magazine, page 31, under "Questions From Readers," the Society claimed that they found out from the 1980 edition of the New Testament by Johannes Greber, that he was involved in spiritism, and therefore they would not quote his bible in the future.

However, the facts are that the Watch Tower Society knew at least from 1956 that Johannes Greber was involved with demon spirits. They published an article to that effect in the *Watchtower* of February 15, 1956. With this knowledge, they deliberately used Greber's "translation" of the Bible as a basis for their *New World Translation of the Holy Scriptures,* which was first released in its entirety in 1961.

Why would the Watch Tower Society knowingly embrace a translation of John 1:1 given by demon spirits? Every Jehovah's Witness needs to check this out. Also, why is the Society still teaching Greber's views on the resurrection received from the same source?

2. *The New Testament in an Improved Version.* Continuing on with the precedents for translating John 1:1, "and the Word was a god," we also find the Watch Tower Society quoting on page 5 of *The Word, Who Is He? According to John,* "This reading is found in *The New Testament in An Improved Version,* published in London, England in 1808."

We are directed to a footnote which reads,

The title page reads: *The New Testament in An Improved Version*, upon the basis of Archbishop Newcome's New Translation: with a corrected Text, and Notes Critical and Explanatory. Published by a Society for Promoting Christian Knowledge and the Practice of Virtue, by the Distribution of Books—Unitarian.

Yes, the key word above is *"Unitarian."* This is a cult group teaching that Jesus was an extraordinarily good man only, nothing more. A Mr. Thos. Belsham, after Archbishop Newcome's death, altered his text (see p. 394, *Manual of Bible Bibliography*). This altered text dishonoring Archbishop Newcome's careful scholarship also provides a basis for the *New World Translation's* "and the Word was a god" (see also the *Kingdom Interlinear Translation* (1969), p. 1160).

Archbishop Newcome certainly never said the Word was "a god." Why would the Watch Tower Society use as their guide a cult denying the biblical Christ and guilty of altering a reputable biblical text? Every Jehovah's Witness needs to check this out.

3. The Emphatic Diaglott by Benjamin Wilson. A third precedent for translation John 1:1 as "and the Word was a god," comes from the *Emphatic Diaglott* by Benjamin Wilson. His translation actually reads, "the *logos* was God," but he placed the words "a god" under *theos* in the Greek and English portion. Mr. Wilson never studied biblical Greek in a college. He was a follower of John Thomas— a proven false prophet by biblical definition and founder of the Christadelphians—a group denying Christ's deity.

A Final Word on John 1:1

All Watch Tower sources for translating John 1:1 as "and the Word was a god" crumble away under close and honest examination. Why would the Watch Tower Society *choose* sources that are false and even demonic? Why do they further *choose* to ignore Greek scholars who are reputable? Every Jehovah's Witness needs to get satisfactory answers to these important questions.

We further suggest a careful reading of chapter 9 on the deity of Jesus Christ so John 1:1 may be understood in its correct context: "In the beginning was the Word, and the Word was with God, and the Word was God."

Misrepresenting Christ Goes On in the New World Translation

A most revealing publication of the Watch Tower Society is a purple interlinear translation called *The Kingdom Interlinear Translation of the Greek Scriptures*, published in 1969. In this book their Scripture distortions can be clearly seen, especially the altering of the text in places where Jesus is called "God." So successful has this publication been in setting Jehovah's Witnesses free from the Watch Tower Society that they have taken it out of print and substituted a navy blue one in which the distortions are masked much more successfully. We recommend the original.

Distortion of Colossians 2:9

"Because it is in him that all the fullness of the divine quality dwells bodily" (NWT). Notice the words "divine quality." They are found nowhere in the Greek text. Why then are they inserted in the *New World Translation*? Obviously because the Jehovah's Witness leaders could not have their membership know that "all the fullness of Deity" is dwelling in Christ bodily! Notice the Greek/English side of the *Kingdom Interlinear Translation*, "Because in him is dwelling down all the fullness of the godship bodily."

Looking up the word "godship" in any reputable Bible dictionary, we find it also reads "Godhead" or "Deity." It can never be honestly translated "divine quality." Why would the Watch Tower translators be so dishonest as to insert extra words in the text and at the same time ignore the truth about Jesus? The correct reading of Colossians 2:9 is "For in Him all the fulness of Deity dwells in bodily form." Yes, all is all, and full is full, and Jesus is deity (God), even in the flesh. No wonder the verse just previous is a warning to watch out for those who would misrepresent Christ:

> See to it that no one takes you captive through philosophy and empty deception, according to the tradition of men, according to the elementary principles of the world, rather than according to Christ (Colossians 2:8).

We need to have the correct doctrine on Jesus Christ, that He is fully deity (God), or we will find ourselves in "empty deception" like the Jehovah's Witnesses.

Misrepresentation of Christ by Ignoring the Context of Scriptures

Much of Jehovah's Witness doctrine is built by using the Bible like a dictionary. You choose your doctrine and then you hunt through the pages of the Bible for a phrase here and a phrase there that will seem to support what you said. Used (or abused) this way, you can make the Bible say just about anything you want it to. Misrepresentation of Christ by ignoring the context is a favorite method of Jehovah's Witnesses as illustrated in the following.

Presenting Jesus as a Creature, "First Created"

Since Jesus is eternal and the Bible teaches this fact, first of all these Scriptures are ignored. The next step is to choose other Scriptures that on the surface seem to teach Jesus is created. Jehovah's Witnesses choose Proverbs 8:22 and 30 after telling the "Bible study" or prospective member that Jesus is created. Then the prospect reads: "Jehovah himself produced me as the beginning of his way, the earliest of his achievements of long ago" (verse 22 NWT) and "Then I came to be beside him as a master worker, and I came to be the one he was specially fond of day by day, I being glad before him all the time" (verse 30 NWT).

Being "primed" in this manner, the prospect assumes that Jesus Christ is the subject of Proverbs 8. However, a study in context reveals that the true subject of Proverbs 8 is "wisdom" personified, and not Jesus Christ at all! Always check the context of the isolated verses misused by Jehovah's Witnesses.

Why not ask the Jehovah's Witness, "If Jehovah created Jesus first, and then Jesus was beside Him as a 'master workman' for the rest of creation as you teach, please explain Isaiah 44:24 to me":

Thus says the LORD [YHWH], your Redeemer,
and the one who formed you from the womb, "I,
the LORD [YHWH], am the maker of all things,

stretching out the heavens *by Myself*, and spreading out the earth *all alone* (emphasis added).

Misrepresenting Christ by Redefining Bible Terms

As with all cult groups, Jehovah's Witnesses lead the way in giving their own meanings to Bible terms. Rather than accepting true definitions which would disprove their doctrines, they invent new meanings. An example is the term "first-born" as applied to Jesus Christ. The Jehovah's Witnesses attempt to use this redefined term to prove that Jesus was created first and so is only a creature. Colossians 1:15 reads in their bible, "He is the image of the invisible God, the first-born of all creation" (NWT).

Here the Scripture is correct, but Jehovah's Witnesses read and teach it with a faulty definition. They equate "first-born" with "first-created," as programmed by the Society.

Notice first of all that this Scripture teaches that Jesus is "the image of the invisible God," not the "creation" of the invisible God. When we look in a mirror, what do we see? An image of ourselves. Is it us? Of course! So Christ is the visible image of the invisible God. Matthew 1:23 calls Him "God with us." Is He then God? Of course!

In the Scripture in Colossians 1:15, Jesus is also called "the first-born of all creation." What does this mean? First off, it does *not* mean "first-created," as the Jehovah Witnesses teach. The word in Greek for "first-created" is *protoktistos*. This term is *never* used in connection with Jesus Christ.

The term "first-born" means in Greek "preeminence in rank." If we just continue reading in Colossians, chapter 1, the meaning becomes clear. Verse 16 says,

> For by Him [Christ] all things were created,
> both in the heavens and on earth, visible and
> invisible, whether thrones or dominions or rulers
> or authorities—all things have been created by
> Him and for Him.

Verse 17 continues, "And He is before all things, and in Him all things hold together."

We rest our case. Jesus Christ is "before all things." That means before the heavens and earth, before angels, before the creation of man. He is the Creator, the one preeminent in rank, the first-born of all creation.

Additional Tampering Necessary to Support Their Distortion

It was necessary for the "translators" of the *New World Translation* to further alter Colossians, chapter 1, to hide the fact that Jesus is the Creator. They dishonestly inserted the word "other" four times in verses 16 and 17 (i.e., "Also, he is before all (other) things . . ." etc.) to prop up their false doctrine that Jesus is a creature.

Micah 5:2 says of Christ, "His goings forth are from long ago, from the days of eternity."

The Hebrew word here for "eternity" is *olam*. No creature is ever described with this word, only God. It is used of YHWH (Jehovah) in Psalm 90:2. God is eternal.

Redefining "Only-Begotten"

Jehovah's Witnesses teach that Jesus was "only-begotten" when Jehovah supposedly created Him in the beginning. Once again, this term has no reference to any so-called creation, and Acts 13:33 even applies this term to the time of Christ's resurrection: "That God has fulfilled this promise to our children in that He *raised up Jesus,* as it is also written in the second Psalm, 'Thou art My Son; today I have begotten Thee'" (emphasis added).

Redefining "Beginning of the Creation of God"

Jehovah's Witnesses quote one phrase of Revelation 3:14: "The beginning of the creation of God" (NWT). This one phrase now becomes a "proof-text" that Jesus was created. However a perusal of several reputable Greek dictionaries produced these definitions for "beginning": "supervisor," "designer," "cause," "origin," and "source." Obviously, in context Jesus is the Creator.

Refusing to Translate Words with Their Primary Meaning

Why would Jehovah's Witness leaders translate the same Greek word for "worship" as "worship" when it applied to the Father, and then change it to "obeisance" when it applied to the Son? It is because they do not want their followers to worship Jesus, for worship belongs to God alone. Followers are then further misled by being told "obeisance" is not really worship.

Reputable Bibles read in Matthew 28:9, "And behold, Jesus met them and greeted them. And they came up and took hold of His feet and worshiped Him." If the disciples— who were Jews and believed in worshiping God alone— worshiped Jesus, then we should follow their example, recognizing Him as God, and worshiping Him also.

Figuratizing the Second Coming of Christ

Christ failed to show up in person first of all in 1874, then in 1914—the dates set by the Jehovah's Witnesses for His visible second coming and the termination of the world. Rather than admit their error and repent, a new doctrine was invented. Scriptures dealing with the visible second coming of Christ were "figuratized" or "spiritualized." That way, they could claim that Christ did "come" in 1914, but *invisibly*!

Matthew 24:3 was altered to read, "What will be the sign of your presence and of the conclusion of the system of things?" (NWT). Altering "coming" to "presence" solved one problem in this false prophecy, but what were they to do with Revelation 1:7? "Look! He is coming with the clouds, and every eye will see him, and those who pierced him; and all the tribes of the earth will beat themselves in grief because of him. Yes, Amen" (NWT).

Why would this Scripture bother saying "Look!" if we couldn't see Him? The embarrassing phrase "every eye will see him" had to be figuratized to mean "eyes of understanding" acquired upon believing the Watch Tower publications. Why then is the Greek word for "eyes" the same as for the "eyes" that Jesus gave sight to when healing a blind person (Matthew 20:34)? Jesus healed literal eyes, and literal eyes will really see Christ at His second coming!

We might add to our list of questions for Jehovah's Witnesses, How exactly will "those who pierced him" see Him, when they teach a soul-sleep/annihilation for the dead, instead of the Bible teaching of a conscious existence after death?

Truly, the altering of Bible texts to try and harmonize them with one's false doctrines presents a never-ending web of deceit. Why not believe the Bible as it is written?

Old Testament Changes

In the *New World Translation*, the Jehovah's Witnesses have "translated" Zechariah 12:10 this way: "And they will certainly look to the One whom they pierced through" (NWT). In this Scripture, Jehovah (YHWH) Himself is speaking, and reliable translations read correctly: "And they will look on Me whom they have pierced."

Yes, Jehovah God Himself says He was pierced through for our transgressions. The Watch Tower Society cannot have their followers knowing that Jesus is Jehovah, and so they altered this text. However they overlooked altering the Scripture that has Jehovah telling us He was sold for 30 pieces of silver, so here it is. It begins with Zechariah speaking:

> Then I said to them: "If it is good in *your* eyes, give (me) my wages; but if not, refrain." And they proceeded to pay my wages, thirty pieces of silver. At that Jehovah said to me: "Throw it to the treasury—that majestic value with which I have been valued from their standpoint. Accordingly I took the thirty pieces of silver and threw it into the treasury at the house of Jehovah" (Zechariah 11:12,13 NWT, emphasis added).

Yes, it was Jehovah God Himself who was valued and sold for 30 pieces of silver, and pierced through for our transgressions, according to His own words. John 19:37 directly applies the Zechariah prophecy to Jesus Christ.

The Watch Tower Society also had to alter Acts 20:28 to read, "Shepherd the congregation of God, which he purchased with the blood of his own (Son)" (NWT). Notice the inserted word (Son) which is not found in any Greek text. It is an addition to suit Watch Tower doctrine. The Scripture in a reliable Bible reads: "Shepherd the church of God, which He purchased with His own blood."

This instruction to the elders is plain enough. It was God's own blood which purchased the church, and any so-called "shepherds" not teaching this truth are simply not true shepherds.

The "Taking in Knowledge" Distortion of John 17:3

Jehovah's Witness leaders needed a Scripture to promote their "Bible studies", which are really studies of their own literature, so they altered John 17:3 to provide one: "This means everlasting life, their *taking in knowledge* of you, the only true God, and of the one whom you sent forth, Jesus Christ" (NWT, emphasis added).

The friendly Witness at your door will then explain that you must "take in knowledge" from their organization to have salvation through the dreadful "battle of Armageddon" coming soon. This Scripture really reads: "And this is eternal life, that they may *know Thee*, the only true God, and Jesus Christ whom Thou has sent" (emphasis added).

Yes, eternal life comes from *knowing* God personally, in the Person of Jesus Christ. A constant studying of Scripture is a good thing, but "taking in knowledge" of itself will not give us eternal life. Jesus Himself stressed this in John 5:39,40: "You search the Scriptures, because you think that in them you have eternal life; and it is these that bear witness of Me; and you are unwilling to come to Me, that you may have life."

No organization can give salvation. A recent *Watchtower*

headlined, "Come to Jehovah's Organization for Salvation," but salvation is only in Jesus Christ, not in any organization.

Twisting the Scriptures on Blood

The entire world reeled in shock when Jim Jones led over 900 people to their deaths in the jungle. I cannot help but wonder how many Jehovah's Witnesses have died without fanfare, one by one, refusing blood transfusions. I was very nearly a statistic also while a Jehovah's Witness. Let's consider this dangerous doctrine.

A key Scripture used by the Jehovah's Witnesses leaders is Genesis 9:4, which they teach is binding on all inhabitants of the earth: "Only flesh with its soul—its blood— you must not eat" (NWT).

This Scripture is telling the flood survivors not to eat unbled meat. Nothing more is implied, except by the Jehovah's Witnesses, who say "eating" means "transfusing." The Old Law Covenant given to the nation of Israel did contain dietary laws on blood, but they were not binding on Gentiles (see Deuteronomy 14:21). Also, Jehovah's Witnesses are taught that they will lose their eternal life if they take a blood transfusion. This excessive penalty for "eating blood" does not even agree with the Old Law Covenant! Here is the penalty contained in Leviticus 17:14,15:

> For the soul of every sort of flesh is its blood by the soul in it. Consequently I said to the sons of Israel: "You must not eat the blood of any sort of flesh, because the soul of every sort of flesh is its blood. Anyone eating it will be cut off." As for any soul that eats a body (already) dead or something torn by a wild beast, whether a native or an alien

resident, he must in that case wash his garments and bathe in water and be unclean until the evening; and he must be clean (NWT).

Yes, the penalty for eating (or in Jehovah's Witness reasoning, taking a blood transfusion) was being "cut off" until you had washed your clothes and taken a bath, and then you could return! Why then believe an organization that would take your eternal life as a penalty for a blood transfusion? God never would.

Likewise, the New Testament Scriptures in Acts, chapter 15, verses 20 and 29, saying among other things to "abstain from blood," are not by any stretch of interpretation referring to blood transfusions.

It is interesting that at one point in the history of the Watch Tower Society all the Scriptures they now use to refuse blood transfusions were used to refuse vaccinations! Remember, that in the past the Society rejected the theory that diseases were caused by germs and ridiculed Pasteur for this scientific truth. The founder of the Society, Charles T. Russell, also taught that appendicitis and typhoid fever were really caused by biting worms in the colon. With their history of advice on medical issues, one would do well to ignore their "truths" on blood transfusions as well.

Linking Up Unrelated Scriptures

In Jehovah's Witness theology, only 144,000 get to go to heaven and have Christ as their mediator. Only a "remnant" of these supposedly remain in heaven (about 9000), and only these can partake of the "Memorial Supper" (communion). They are the elite class. The rest of the Jehovah's Witnesses must look to this group to be their "mediator" between them and God, and are only allowed to be "other sheep" and live on the earth.

As you can well imagine, it took quite a lot of scriptural manipulation to come up with this doctrine. Revelation, chapter 7, which is a heavenly scene from beginning to end when read in context, had to be divided into heavenly and earthly. As an example, let's consider one verse, Revelation 7:4: "And I heard the number of those who were sealed, one hundred and forty-four thousand sealed from every tribe of the sons of Israel."

A Jehovah's Witness is expected to take the number 144,000 *literally*, but the following phrase: "sealed from every tribe of the sons of Israel" *figuratively*. This allows for the Watch Tower doctrine of 144,000 Jehovah's Witnesses (spiritual Israelites) to form the "little flock" with a heavenly hope and the rest, the "great crowd," to have an earthly hope obtained by obeying the "little flock." The context of the Scripture is ignored.

The valid Bible term "little flock" used in Luke 12:32 was redefined to mean the remnant of this 144,000 heavenly class when read: "Have no fear, little flock, because *your* Father has approved of giving *you* the Kingdom" (NWT, emphasis added).

This misinterpretation allows the "remnant" or governing members at Watch Tower headquarters to rule over the others since they alone receive the "kingdom" from the Father, and all others get it only through them as the mediators. Christ also becomes the mediator only for this "little flock," and they are the "mediators" for the rest.

What is the correct context of the term "little flock"? When Jesus spoke these words, He was speaking to the small gathering of converted Jewish believers. He called them His "little flock." Jesus went on to say in John 10:16, "And I have other sheep, which are not of this fold; those also I must bring, and they will listen to my voice, and they will become one flock, one shepherd" (NWT).

Was Jesus here speaking of a secondary, earthly class who would join with the "little flock" and look to them for salvation, as the Jehovah's Witnesses teach? No, Jesus was speaking of the time when the door to the kingdom would be opened to the Gentiles also. His words were fulfilled during the account in Acts 11:1-18. Paul wrote also of the fulfillment of Jesus' words in Galatians 3:28,29:

> There is neither Jew nor Greek, there is neither slave nor free man, there is neither male nor female; for you are all one in Christ Jesus. And if you belong to Christ, then you are Abraham's offspring, heirs according to promise.

When read in context the Scriptures do not support the Jehovah's Witness doctrine of heavenly/earthly hopes. There will be a "new heavens and a new earth" arrangement as promised in the Bible, but it bears no resemblance to the Watch Tower one. Revelation chapters 21–22 give the biblical description of the "new heavens and new earth" arrangement.

Witnessing to Jehovah's Witnesses at Your Door

Do not attempt to pray with the Jehovah's Witnesses (this offends them), but do pray before they come or before you speak with them. In Jesus' name, ask for the anointing of the Holy Spirit to help you witness effectively. Pray also that the Holy Spirit will convict the Jehovah's Witnesses of their errors.

Listen politely to their presentation of three or four Scriptures, and do not enter into an argument or discussion. Let them make their point, even if it is incorrect, and when they look to you for a response, just smile and say "please go on." This will ensure that they will quickly finish and offer you the literature.

When offered the literature, say something like, "You people have come to my home because you really believe you are in the true faith. I also believe I am in the true faith, and yet we believe differently. I think we should take a moment to take the Bible test as to whether we are in the true faith or not." Have a Bible handy and marked at 2 Corinthians 13:5, which reads, "Test yourselves to see if you are in the faith; examine yourselves! Or do you not recognize this about yourselves, that *Jesus Christ is in you*—unless indeed you fail the test?" (emphasis added).

Explain to them that you know you are in the true faith because you have Jesus Christ within you, and then share your testimony with them. If they interrupt, remind them that you listened politely to them while they shared, so they should quietly listen to you.

They may object that their *New World Translation* says in this Scripture that Jesus Christ is "in union with" you, not "in you." This is a perfect time to direct them to their *Kingdom Interlinear Translation* so they can check out the English words under the Greek and learn about the indwelling Christ firsthand.

Attempt to exchange literature. Some will do this, some won't. If they refuse to take Christian literature written especially for them, invite them to return and answer your questions. Then take the tract you planned to give them and write out some of the points in your own handwriting. This takes a little of your time, but souls are precious.

Remember always that the Jehovah's Witnesses at your door went into that organization because they were honestly seeking for God in their hearts. They were given instead a counterfeit Christ and a counterfeit gospel. They unknowingly carry an unreliable Bible. They are busy and programmed, but they are still hungry in the deepest part of their hearts, and with the help of the Holy Spirit and a proper Bible, you can reach them for Christ. Remember to pray for them.

Chapter 3

EXPOSING MORMONISM
(THE CHURCH OF JESUS CHRIST
OF LATTER-DAY SAINTS)

The Church of Jesus Christ of Latter-day Saints, the Mormons, rises or falls on Joseph Smith, their prophet. They believe there is no salvation without accepting him (see *Doctrines of Salvation*, vol. 1, p. 189).

There are many divisions in the Mormon church, numbering over 100 sects—all claiming to be the true church based on the prophet, Joseph Smith. The largest is headquartered in Salt Lake City, Utah. We need to examine Joseph Smith, obviously, and see if his claims to be a prophet of God hold up.

Joseph Smith and His Visions

Joseph Smith Jr. as a young man had a series of visions. The basis of the Mormon church is belief in these visions of their prophet. In a pamphlet distributed publicly by the Mormon elders (missionaries) called *The Prophet Joseph Smith's Testimony*, the reader is told that Joseph Smith was 14 years old in 1820. He saw *two* personages in his vision: God the Father and God the Son.

When the light rested upon me I saw two

personages, whose brightness and glory defy all description. One of them spake unto me, calling me by name, and said, pointing to the other—"This is My Beloved Son, Hear Him!"

This most recent version of the vision suits the present Mormon doctrine of plural gods, but Joseph Smith told several other versions of the same story down through the years. On file at Brigham Young University, and included in the "Brigham Young University Studies, Spring 1969," page 281, there is a document suppressed for 130 years. This document was "the only known account of the Vision" in Joseph Smith's own handwriting, predating the official church version by six years (see *Dialogue; A Journal of Mormon Thought*, Spring 1971, p. 86).

Why is disclosure of this earlier vision so damning to the church? Because the church says officially that Joseph was 14, but Joseph says in his own handwriting that he was 16. The church says he saw two personages, the Father and Son. Joseph says in his own handwriting that "I saw the Lord." This *one* personage, the Lord, went on to say, "Behold I am the Lord of glory. I was crucified." Interested Mormons should do their own research right at Brigham Young University.

The Origin of the Book of Mormon

The Mormon church today claims that Joseph Smith found gold plates buried in the hill Cumorah, which he later translated using the "urim and thummin." The urim and thummin are believed to be precious stones which were located in the breastplate of the high priest of Israel, according to some Bible scholars. Nowhere in the Bible were they used to translate anything as the Mormons claim. The *Book of Mormon* was published in 1830 with the statement that it was "the fullness of the everlasting gospel." Some 3900 changes have been made to this "fullness" since 1830, not counting punctuation. As well, other "inspired" books have been added, namely *Doctrine and Covenants* and *Pearl of Great Price.*

We have provided a chart at the end of this chapter called "Contradictory Mormon Doctrine" which shows how all these so-called "inspired" books contrast with each other. Since Mormons claim that the King James Version of the Bible is inspired, we have included this also. No Mormon presented with this chart has had an explanation for us, but it does raise many questions for them.

What Mormons Really Believe

Mormons go to great lengths to appear "Christian" when presenting Mormonism, and representatives from the Church of Jesus Christ of Latter-day Saints keep their true doctrine well-hidden when calling in your home. The Latter-day Saints church has even added a phrase to the *Book of Mormon.* It now has a subtitle, "Another Testament of Jesus Christ," to make it appear as a companion to the Bible.

The missionary elders won't tell you that they are the only true church and believe all others are of the devil. They won't tell you that they hope to be gods themselves one day, even being exalted to "God the Father" of their own planet, where they will carry on celestial sex with plural wives, in order to populate an earth of their own and thereby receive the worship of their creation.

They won't disclose one detail of their secret temple rites, nor will they reveal that they are wearing special temple underwear to protect themselves from non-Mormons like you. They won't tell you that their temple ceremony has been recently changed due, we believe, to the public exposing of their occultic and offensive rituals taking place behind closed doors.

Most importantly, they won't tell you that they are misrepresenting Jesus Christ, although His name figures prominently in their church name. They believe Jesus to be a spirit-brother of Lucifer (the devil), and only one of many gods. Early Mormon leaders taught that Jesus was a polygamous husband to both the Marys and Martha, and had offspring. This teaching has never been corrected to date.

Was Joseph Smith a True Prophet of God?

Joseph Smith had a rather high opinion of himself, as evidenced by this statement from *History of the Church* (vol. 6, pp. 408-09, 1844):

> I have more to boast of than any man had. I am the only man that has been able to keep a whole church together since the days of Adam. A large majority of the whole have stood by me. Neither Paul, John, Peter, nor Jesus ever did it. I boast that no man ever did such a work as I. The followers of Jesus ran away from him, but the Latter-day Saints never ran away from me yet.

Joseph Smith thought at least as highly of himself as many modern-day Mormons think of him. Is he indeed a prophet of God as claimed by the Mormon church, or was he a false prophet, as many researchers believe?

The Bible Test for a Prophet

The Bible outlines a clear test for those who would be prophets of God. Deuteronomy 18:20-22 records:

> But the prophet, which shall presume to speak a word in my name, which I have not commanded him to speak, or that shall speak in the name of other gods, even that prophet shall die. And if thou say in thine heart, How shall we know the word which the Lord hath not spoken? When a prophet speaketh in the name of the Lord, if the thing follow not, nor come to pass, that is the thing which the Lord hath not spoken, but the prophet hath spoken it presumptuously; thou shall not be afraid of him (KJV).

Listed below are a few examples of Joseph Smith's failed prophecies:

1830: In the Book of Mormon, 2 Nephi 30:6, a prophecy is recorded promising that the Lamanites (Native Indians of America) would turn "white and delightsome" within a few generations of accepting the (Mormon) gospel. By 1981 it was evident that none had changed color, and so this prophecy was altered in the *Book of Mormon* to read, "pure and delightsome."

1832: Joseph Smith prophesied that the New Jerusalem would be built on the temple lot in Missouri, stating, "This generation shall not all pass away until an house shall be built unto the Lord" (see *Doctrine and Covenants* 84:2-5,31.) Joseph Smith passed away, his generation passed away, and no temple was built. Later attempts by the church to say a generation was 100 years long also proved false by 1932. In fact, the temple lot is still empty and is not even owned by the Church of Jesus Christ of Latter-day Saints headquartered in Salt Lake City, but is owned by a splinter group of "Temple Lot" Mormons, and to date, they aren't selling!

1835: Joseph Smith prophesied "the coming of the Lord, which was nigh—even 56 years should wind up the scene" (*History of the Church*, vol. 2, p. 182). The Lord should have therefore arrived according to Joseph Smith's prophecy in 1835 plus 56 years or 1891. Joseph Smith also said on another occasion that "the Son of Man will not come in the clouds of heaven till I am eighty-five years old" (*Joseph Smith's Teachings* by E.F. Parry, p. 86).

Not only did the Lord fail to show up in 1891, but Joseph Smith did not live to be 85 years old. He was killed on July 27, 1944, while being held in jail for adultery and wrecking the press of the *Nauvoo Expositor* newspaper. Joseph Smith is, in fact, presented as a martyr to the Mormon people, supposedly sealing his testimony with his blood. The facts are, however, that Joseph Smith died in a blazing Old West gun battle, but not before he had killed two men and injured a third. While not mentioned publicly, this is recorded in *History of the Church*, vol. 5, pp. 616-18.

As stated earlier, the Mormon church rises or falls on Joseph Smith and his claims to be a prophet. He fails the test of the Bible prophet, and therefore the whole organization is faulty.

Presenting the Gospel to Mormons

A Christian needs to prepare before an encounter with

the Mormons by praying. Realize that you will be in a spiritual battle for their souls, so you must be prepared spiritually. Remember that Mormons have had an emotional experience called "burning in the bosom" that Mormonism is true, and facts take second place to this experience.

If possible, you should pray before the Mormons arrive. Mormons will want to lead in prayer, but it is not proper for a Christian to bow his head while the Mormons pray since they are praying to a "heavenly Father" who is an exalted man of flesh and bones with numerous wives. This is not the heavenly Father of the Bible or Christianity. The Mormons are usually agreeable to you praying, so do so in addition to your earlier praying.

We believe Christians should be polite but noncommittal while the Mormons go through their presentation. Just say "please go on" if they attempt to make you agree. At the end they will try and place a *Book of Mormon* with you with marked passages for you to consider and pray about whether it is true or not, explaining that your "bosom will burn" if you do this. Believe it or not, this is how most persons embrace Mormonism.

Thank the missionaries for their offer to leave the *Book of Mormon* in your home, but ask them, "Don't you believe that the *Book of Mormon* has a familiar spirit?" They will usually answer yes. If they are uncertain, tell them to ask their bishop or refer them to *A Marvellous Work and a Wonder*, pages 67 and 68 (a Mormon publication). Tell them that since the *Book of Mormon* has a familiar spirit, you must decline to have it in your home due to Leviticus 19:31. Invite them to read this from their Bible (always a King James Version): "Regard not them that have familiar spirits; neither seek after wizards, to be defiled by them; I am the Lord your God" (KJV).

Explain to them that "familiar spirits" are always of the devil and never from God, and since by their own admission their *Book of Mormon* has a "familiar spirit," you do not wish to disobey the Bible and defile your home. If they remain, share your personal testimony.

Discussing the "Burning in the Bosom" Experience

Thank the Mormons for their testimony that "the Mormon church is true," etc. which they all present in a well-rehearsed manner and is based mainly on the same "burning in the bosom" experience they have asked you to participate in.

Invite them to turn to Luke 24. Beginning in verse 13, we have the account of two disciples (point out that they were believers already, not unbelievers) on the road to Emmaus. The account goes on to say that the risen Christ joined them, keeping their eyes "holden" so they would not immediately recognize Him (verse 16). Jesus explained the Scriptures and their fulfillment to these two disciples. By verses 31 and 32, we have this development,

> And their eyes were opened, and they knew him; and he vanished out of their sight. And they said one to another, Did not our heart burn [bosoms burn] within us, while he talked with us by the way, and while he opened to us the scriptures? (KJV).

Now point out to the Mormons that this "burning in the bosom" is not for unbelievers to see if Mormonism is true but was an experience for believing disciples, which happened when they understood Jesus' explanation of the

Scriptures. It did not come after praying for it. Therefore you would not seek after an experience that the Bible does not command. However, point out that John 3 does have a command for those who would *know* Christ, and that even religious persons like Nicodemus need to obey this command: "Do not marvel that I said to you, 'You must be born again'" (John 3:7).

Share your experience of being personally "born again" in Christ, and pray after they leave that the Holy Spirit will convict them. Remember that many of the young Mormon missionaries do not fully understand their own doctrine and are not well versed in the Bible. Usually they pair off a strong one with a weaker one. Many times our efforts to reach them with the gospel do not get immediate results but will bear fruit in the future. Continue to pray.

Contradictory Mormon Doctrine*

Question	Mormon Scripture Says	Contrasting Mormon Scripture Says	King James Bible
Is God an exalted man?	*No!* "Believest thou that this Great Spirit, who is God, created all things" (Alma 18:28 BoM).	*Yes!* "The Father has a body of flesh and bones as tangible as man's the Son also" (D&C 130:22).	*No!* "God is a Spirit" (John 4:24); "God is not a man" (Numbers 23:19).
Are the Father, Son, and the Holy Ghost *one God?*	*Yes!* "Which Father, Son and Holy Ghost are one God, infinite and eternal" (D&C 20:28).	*No!* "Father, Son, and Holy Ghost comprise the Godhead. As each of these persons is a God...a plurality of God exists" (M.D., pp. 576-77).	*Yes!* "For there are three that bear record in heaven, the Father, the Word, and the Holy Ghost, and these three are one" (1 John 5:7).
Is God eternal?	*Yes!* "For I know that God is not a partial God, neither a changeable being; but he is unchangeable from all eternity to all eternity" (Moroni 8:18 BoM).	*No!* "We have imagined and supposed that God was God from all eternity. I will refute that idea" (M.D., p. 321).	*Yes!* "The eternal God is thy refuge" (Deuteronomy 33:27).

* Abbreviations used: D&C—*Doctrine and Covenants*   M.D.—*Mormon Doctrine* by Bruce R. McConkie
PGP—*Pearl of Great Price*   BoM—*Book of Mormon*

Question	Mormon Scripture Says	Contrasting Mormon Scripture Says	King James Bible
Does God change?	*No!* "There is a God in heaven who is infinite and eternal, from everlasting to everlasting, the same unchangeable God" (D&C 20:17).	*Yes!* "We believe in a God who is Himself progressive ...whose perfection consists in eternal advancement" (*Articles of Faith*, p. 430).	*No!* "For I am the LORD, I change not" (Malachi 3:6).
Is there a plurality of Gods?	*No!* "The Father and the Son and the Holy Ghost are one ...and whoso shall declare more or less than this, and establish it for my doctrine, the same cometh of evil" (3 Nephi 11:27,40 BoM).	*Yes!* "These three are the only Gods we worship. But in addition there is an infinite number of holy personages, drawn from worlds without number, who ...are gods" (M.D., p. 576-77).	*No!* "I am he; before me there was no God formed, neither shall there be after me" (Isaiah 43:10).
Can men be gods?	*No!* "Now Zeezrom said: Is there more than one God? And he answered, No" (Alma 11:28,29 BoM).	*Yes!* "Then shall they (those resurrected) be gods, because they have no end" (D&C 132:20).	*No!* "Thus saith the LORD ...beside me there is no God" (Isaiah 44:6).
Did God create man?	*Yes!* "And I, God, created man in mine own image" (Moses 2:27, PGP).	*No!* "Man was also in the beginning with God ...For man is spirit" (D&C 93:29,33).	*Yes!* "And the Lord God formed man" (Genesis 2:7).

Question	Mormon Scripture Says	Contrasting Mormon Scripture Says	King James Bible
Can God be seen?	*No!* "For without this (the authority of the priesthood) no man can see the face of God, even the Father and live" (D&C 84:22). (J. Smith did not have priesthood when he claimed to see God.)	*Yes!* "And he (Moses) saw God face to face, and he talked with him....Moses could endure his presence" (Moses 1:2, PGP).	*No!* "No man hath seen God at any time; the only begotten Son...hath declared him" (John 1:18).
Is Jesus the one true God?	*Yes!* "Blessed be the name of the Most High God. And they did fall down at the feet of Jesus and did worship him" (3 Nephi 11:17, BoM).	*No!* "Jesus Christ a separate and distinct personage ...three distinct personages and three gods" (*Teachings of the Prophet Joseph Smith* by J.F. Smith, p. 370).	*Yes!* "Now unto the King eternal, immortal, invisible, the only wise God" (speaking of Jesus Christ— 1 Timothy 1:17).
Is Jesus Christ eternal?	*Yes!* "From all eternity to all eternity, the Great I AM, even Jesus Christ" (D&C 39:1).	*No!* "Christ, the First-born, was the mightiest of all the spirit children of the Father" (M.D., p. 590).	*Yes!* "Whose goings forth have been...from everlasting" (Micah 5:2).

Question	Mormon Scripture Says	Contrasting Mormon Scripture Says	King James Bible
Was Jesus born of a virgin?	*Yes!* "And behold, he shall be born of Mary at Jerusalem...she being a virgin" (Alma 7:10, BoM).	*No!* "Christ was begotten by an Immortal Father in the same way that mortal men are begotten by mortal fathers" (M.D, p. 547).	*Yes!* "When as his mother Mary was espoused to Joseph, before they came together, she was found with child" (Matthew 1:18).
Is Jesus the way to salvation?	*Yes!* "Behold, Jesus Christ is the name...there is none other name whereby man can be saved" (D&C 18:23).	*No!* "The President of the Church of Jesus Christ of Latter-day Saints holds the keys of salvation for all men now living" (M.D., p. 411).	*Yes!* "One mediator between God and men, the man Christ Jesus" (1 Timothy 2:5).
Does Christ's blood cleanse us from all sin?	*Yes!* "Salvation was, and is, and is to come, in and through the atoning blood of Christ, the Lord Omnipotent" (Mosiah 3:18 BoM).	*No!* "For the blood of Christ alone under certain circumstances will not avail (for atonement of sins)" (M.D., p. 93).	*Yes!* "And the blood of Jesus Christ his Son cleanseth us from all sin" (1 John 1:7).
Is salvation by grace, not works?	*Yes!* "And we know that justification through the grace of our Lord and Saviour, is just and true" (D&C 20:30).	*No!* "That by keeping the commandments they might be washed and cleansed from all their sins" (D&C 76:52).	*Yes!* "For by grace are ye saved through faith; and that not of yourselves; it is the gift of God; not of works" (Ephesians 2:8,9).

Question	Mormon Scripture Says	Contrasting Mormon Scripture Says	King James Bible
Is there salvation after death?	*No!* "For behold, if ye have procrastinated the day of your repentance even until death . . . the devil hath all power over you; and this is the final state of the wicked" (Alma 34:35 BoM).	*Yes!* "In relation to the dead . . . For their salvation is necessary and essential to our salvation . . . that they without us cannot be made perfect" (D&C 128:15).	*No!* "And as it is appointed unto men once to die, but after this the judgment" (Hebrews 9:27).
Is hell everlasting destruction?	*Yes!* "Yea, they were encircled about by the bands of death, and the chains of hell, and an everlasting destruction did await them" (Alma 5:7 BoM).	*No!* "Whosoever, therefore receives God's punishment receives eternal punishment, whether it is endured one hour, one day, one week, one year or an age" (*Plan of Salvation*, p. 30—pamphlet distributed by elders).	*Yes!* "And the smoke of their torment ascendeth up for ever and ever; and they have no rest day nor night" (Revelation 14:11).

Truly, Mormonism is full of contradictions, even in its own recognized writings. Its claim to be Christian is false, and this is evident by a study of statements contained in these charts. Mormonism is not Christianity!

A Comparison

Topic	Mormonism	Christianity
The Preexistence of Jesus Christ	The Mormon Jesus was born in the heavens as a spirit-child of a "heavenly father" named Elohim, an exalted man, and one of his spirit-wives by sexual relations. Lucifer, who became Satan the Devil, is the brother of this Mormon Jesus (*The Gospel Through the Ages*, p. 15; *History of the Church*, vol. 6, pp. 397, 474).	Jesus Christ is not created, but is eternal, and has always been God (see 1 Timothy 1:16,17; John 1:1-3; Micah 5:2; 1 Timothy 3:16; Titus 2:13, Revelation 1:8; Matthew 1:23).
The Earthly Birth of Jesus Christ	Elohim, the Mormon heavenly father, came to this earth in human form and had sex relations with the Virgin Mary, who was then no longer a virgin. She gave birth to the Mormon Jesus as a result (see *Doctrines of Salvation*, vol. 1:18; Orson Pratt, *The Seer*, p. 158; and *Journal of Discourses* 8:115, quoting Brigham Young).	Jesus Christ was born of the virgin Mary as "Emmanuel," "God with us" (see Matthew 1:23). Jesus was conceived in the Virgin Mary's womb when the Holy Spirit came upon her (see Matthew 1:20).
The Earthly Life of Jesus Christ	The Mormon Jesus was the bridegroom at Cana of Galilee according to the Mormon interpretation of John 2:1-12, and was therefore married to at least one wife while on earth (see *Journal of Discourses*, vol. 2, p. 82, quoting Orson Hyde [Apostle]).	There is no biblical record of Jesus' marrying. A reading of the account in John 2:1-12 shows that Jesus was "invited" to the wedding. Bridegrooms do not receive invitations to their own weddings!

Topic	Mormonism	Christianity
Your Mother Which Art in Heaven? Mrs. God?	Mormonism teaches that God the Father has many wives in heaven, thereby resulting in not only a father in heaven, but a mother-in-heaven Mormon doctrine. All Mormons on earth today believe they were originally the result of such a sexual, heavenly union (see Orson Pratt, *The Seer*, p. 37; also *Mormon Doctrine* by Bruce McConkie, p. 516).	The Bible has absolutely no mention of any such "wives" of God the Father.
View of the Bible	"Ignorant translators, careless subscribers, or designing and corrupt priests have committed many errors—many plain and precious things were deleted, in consequence of which error and falsehood poured into the various churches. One of the great heresies of modern Christendom is the unfounded assumption that the Bible contains all of the inspired teachers now extant among man" (*Mormon Doctrine*, pp. 82,83).	"All scripture is given by inspiration of God, and is profitable for doctrine, for reproof, for correction, for instruction in righteousness; that the man of God may be perfect, thoroughly furnished unto all good works" (2 Timothy 3:16,17 KJV). "Thy word is very pure" (Psalm 119:140).
Baptism for the Dead and Genealogy	Mormons research genealogies and get baptized in their temples in proxy for their dead relatives. They misinterpret 1 Corinthians 15:29, "Else what shall they do which are baptized for the dead, if the dead rise not at all? Why are they then baptized for the dead?" (KJV).	Doing genealogies is useless for the Christian (see 1 Timothy 1:3,4). First Corinthians, chapter 15, is on the subject of the resurrection, not baptism. First Corinthians 15:29 shows the folly of *those* (not *we* believers, but *those* unbelievers) who denied the resurrection, and yet practiced the pagan rite

Topic	Mormonism	Christianity
		of "baptism for the dead." Hebrews 9:27 shows that once a person is dead, he faces judgment. Nothing the living do changes this.
View of the Church	"There is no salvation outside the Church of Jesus Christ of Latter-day Saints" (*Mormon Doctrine*, p. 670). "All other churches are entirely destitute of all authority from God; and any person who receives Baptism or the Lord's Supper from their hands will highly offend God; for He looks upon them as the most corrupt of all people. Both Catholics and Protestants are nothing less than the whore of Babylon" (*The Seer*, p. 255).	The church in the Bible is the entire born-again body of believers in the true Jesus Christ of the Bible (Almighty God manifest in the flesh). It is not a manmade organization with a false prophet at its head! The true church partakes of the Lord's Supper of bread and wine, not water as the Mormons use (see John 3:3-7; Ephesians 1:22,23; 4:11-16; Matthew 26:26-30).

In Conclusion: As will be evident by this time, Mormonism is not Christianity. Further, Mormonism has made attacks against the body of Christ in all denominations. This is an honest attempt to defend the true gospel of Jesus Christ and point out the errors of those coming to us preaching another Jesus, another gospel, with a different spirit (see 2 Corinthians 11:4). Jesus Christ is Lord!

Chapter 4

A LOOK AT SEVENTH-DAY ADVENTISM

There are now two distinct camps in Adventism. The split became apparent in the late 1970s when pastors of many years' standing began to question their prophetess, Ellen G. White. They began to question her peculiar doctrines which could not be supported fully by the Scriptures. Many were disillusioned by the revelation of her plagiarism, which was very extensive and documented in the book *The White Lie* by former Seventh-day Adventist pastor, Walter Rea.

The hundreds of pastors who questioned Ellen White as an absolute authority and discovered the cover-up by the White Estate soon found themselves on the outside, still trying to bring about reform from that disadvantaged position. Two camps quickly formed: those loyal to Ellen White, and those determined to be loyal to the Bible above all else.

The Seventh-day Adventist church "felt the heat" and formed councils to look into Ellen White's peculiar doctrines. They have spent years in discussion, published endless papers, but have not corrected Ellen White's views. Therefore, since an adequate time period has passed for

57

these issues to be corrected by the church, we must again take a look at Adventism as it stands today and decide: Is it Christian or a cult? We must examine Ellen G. White as she relates to the Seventh-day Adventist church today.

Ellen G. White—Her Visions and Writings

Recently, a general mailing was done by the Seventh-day Adventists to pastors of various Christian churches. Pastors received free of charge a book called *Seventh-day Adventists Believe...A Biblical Exposition of 27 Fundamental Doctrines* (March 1989). Upon reading the book, designed to make Seventh-day Adventism look evangelical and fundamental, one nevertheless eventually comes to the section on Ellen G. White, beginning on page 224.

Here the Seventh-day Adventists begin listing several points continuing through page 228 as to why they believe the "gift of prophecy was active in the ministry of Ellen G. White, one of the founders of the Seventh-day Adventist Church." They pose the question on page 224, "How does Ellen White's ministry measure against the Biblical tests of a prophet?"

A good question, indeed, and we will add our observations based on years of research to their carefully selected comments. We hope we will not offend if we speak plainly. We may be revealing things modern Seventh-day Adventists did not realize, but all quotes are documented and are true. We also merely want to put Ellen G. White to the biblical tests of a prophet to see if she measures up, as this book suggests we do.

1. *We read in their publication that Ellen G. White's writings are in agreement with the Bible* (p. 224): "Her

writings are consistent, accurate, and in full agreement with the Scriptures."

We must take issue with all three descriptions. First, her writings are not consistent. We will give only one example, due to limited space. We will briefly outline her "visions" on the "shut door" doctrine (a major doctrine), and see how "consistent" she was.

Briefly, this was the teaching that the door to salvation was closed by the bridegroom (Jesus Christ), based on the parable of Matthew 25:1-13, on October 22, 1844. Early Adventists, including Ellen G. White, believed they were inside and all others were shut out and cut off. They saw themselves as the "wise virgins" (safely inside with Christ) and all the others as "foolish virgins" (left outside the shut door).

When Christ did not come for His "wise virgins" on the prophesied date in 1844, Ellen White attempted to cover over her support of this false prophecy by the following statement in *Selected Messages* (vol. 1, p. 63):

> For a time after the disappointment in 1844, I did hold, in common with the advent body that the door of mercy was then forever closed to the world. This position was taken before my first vision was given me. It was the light given me of God that corrected our error, and enabled us to see the true position.

So Ellen White excused her support of a false prophecy by saying it occurred before her first vision, and that her first vision corrected the error. But did it? Modern-day Adventists might be interested in a portion of her first vision, claimed for December 1844 (which phrase is now conveniently deleted) which does indeed support the "shut door" theory. Remember, the "vision" was a judgment on the "apostates," the early Adventists, and others who doubted her visions: "It was just as impossible for them to get on the path again and go to the City, as all the wicked world which God had rejected." Rather than "correcting" the "shut door" prophecy as claimed, the first vision supports it!

In reference to her second vision, Ellen White spoke of her suffering over those who would not accept the "shut door":

> Many of them did not believe in a shut door . . . unbelief seemed to be on every hand. . . . There was one sister there. . . . She had great sympathy, and could not believe the door was shut. . . . I felt very, very, sad. . . . Most of them received the vision (from EGW) and were settled upon the shut door" (letter B-3-1847 to Joseph Bates, July 13, 1847, White Estate).

We could continue on, but the facts are that Ellen White taught the "shut door" theory for at least six years after she claimed she did not. To cover up this inconsistency in her writings, the Seventh-day Adventist church redefined the meaning of "shut door" and carefully deleted all her references to it. Is this consistent? Is this honest?

Are her visions and writings accurate as claimed? No, we do not believe so. Especially in the area of health reform she strayed far from accuracy, all the while claiming her insight came from God. In *Selected Messages* (vol. 3, p. 75, editions may vary), she said, "The gospel includes health reform in all its phases." She then went on to state that if we ate meat from animals we would take on their nature: "If we subsist largely upon the flesh of dead animals, we shall partake of their nature" (*Counsels on Diet and Foods*, p. 390, editions may vary).

The Bible does not teach such nonsense. Jesus Himself ate fish and lamb. Paul stated in 1 Corinthians 10:25, "Eat anything that is sold in the meat market, without asking questions for conscience' sake."

The further claim is made that her writings are "in full agreement with the Scriptures." To this sweeping statement we must ask the following questions. Just where in Scripture do we find that "He (Adam) was more than twice as tall as men now living upon the earth" (*Spiritual Gifts*, vol. 3, p. 34, editions may vary)?

Where in the Scriptures do we find this "truth" as revealed by Ellen White in *Early Writings* (first edition, pp. 30 and 32): "All the angels that are commissioned to visit the earth hold a golden card, which they present to the angel at the gates of the city as they pass in and out"?

The list could go on, but we believe the point is adequately made. We have accepted the Seventh-day Adventist challenge to put Ellen G. White to the test on point one and we have found that she is not consistent, accurate, nor is she in agreement with the Scriptures on many important points. She fails this test.

2. *The book* Seventh-day Adventists Believe *goes on to say of Ellen White that she is reliable due to the accuracy of predictions.* There are two instances cited: the rise of modern spiritualism, and close cooperation between Protestants and Roman Catholics.

The two instances chosen above for "accuracy of predictions" are vague and set no dates, but we agree are generally true. However, there are other more specific predictions not cited that were false. For example, referring to 1844:

> I saw the state of the different churches since the second angel proclaimed their fall. They have been growing more and more corrupt. . . . Satan has taken full possession of the churches as a body. . . . Their professions, their prayers and their exhortations are an abomination in the sight of God" (*Spiritual Gifts*, vol. 1, p. 189).

If this prediction is true, and since 1844 all churches are possessed of the devil, why are the Seventh-day Adventists trying so hard to appear as evangelical Christians and join in ministerial associations? Why bother with the expense of sending out a book?

Here is another false prediction contained in *Testimony for the Church*, p. 255: "The system of slavery, which ruined our nation, is left to live and stir up another rebellion." Is the United States "ruined" as a nation? Is slavery still left for another "rebellion"?

We agree that her predictions were not many, but if even one fails, she is by biblical definition a false prophet.

The Adventist publication would have us believe that "fruits" are the proof of a true or false prophet, but that is not so. Proof of fulfillment is proof of a prophet, true or false. Since they liken her to Jeremiah, they should judge her by Scriptures pertaining to prophets. For example, the entire twenty-third chapter of Jeremiah refers to prophets, but we will quote only one verse, Jeremiah 23:32, as an example:

> "Behold, I am against those who have prophesied false dreams," declares the Lord, "and related them, and led My people astray by their falsehoods and reckless boasting; yet I did not

send them or command them, nor do they furnish this people the slightest benefit," declares the Lord.

3. *The Seventh-day Adventist publication goes on to say of Ellen G. White that she is true because she gives the acknowledgement of Christ's incarnation.* We must agree with the brief statement contained on Christ, that He is fully God and fully man. We cannot agree, however, that she is the author of *Desire of Ages* as claimed. The extent of her plagiarism is now well-known, and we recommend every Adventist read *The White Lie* by former pastor Walter Rea. The church has yet to reply to his challenge to prove that even 20 percent of her writings are her own! The fact that copyright laws were not strict in her day does not excuse her "borrowing."

What this section does not tell you is that Adventists also believe that Jesus Christ is Michael. They are quick to point out that they do not believe Jesus is any kind of an angel. Since Michael is called an "archangel," they interpret this to mean that Jesus is "chief over the angels," while still being God. However Daniel 10:13 says that Michael is "one of the chief princes." Jesus is not "one of" any group! Michael lacked the authority to rebuke Satan (Jude 9). Jesus, on the other hand, repeatedly rebuked Satan (Matthew 17:18; Mark 9:25; etc.). Jesus is clearly not Michael.

Again, referring to the book distributed by the Seventh-day Adventists, we find the heading on page 227, "The Spirit of Prophecy and the Bible." Here the statement is made that "The writings of Ellen White are not a substitute for Scripture. They cannot be placed on the same level."

This, of course, is what they want evangelical churches to think, but their other publications give a far different view of her writings. *Ministry* magazine, October 1981, contained many startling statements, not the least of which was this one on page 8:

> We believe the revelation and inspiration of both the Bible and Ellen White's writings to be of equal quality. The superintendence of the Holy Spirit was just as careful and thorough in one case as in the other.

This quotation pretty well sums up their view under the remaining points on pages 227 and 228 of *Seventh-day Adventists Believe*. A careful reading of this section shows how extreme is their devotion to and belief in their prophetess, even going so far as to say that she had "the spirit of prophecy" referred to in Revelation.

In closing, they invite the reader to "test everything." We have done our best to do just that. We believe the Seventh-day Adventist church could perhaps one day be evangelical, but only when it rids itself of the influence of Ellen G. White and corrects some of its views on Jesus Christ and salvation.

The Seventh-day Sabbath

Seventh-day Adventists strive to keep "the law" of the Old Testament. They place emphasis on the Ten Commandments as "the law," when in fact the Ten Commandments form only a small part of the entire law. Saturday Sabbath-keeping is greatly stressed as a requirement for salvation in this extremely legalistic group.

Seventh-day Adventists have a habit of thinking "Ten Commandments" or "Sabbath" every time the Bible mentions "the law." This is not correct. The word "law" occurs over 400 times in Scripture, and refers to the entire law, comprising ceremonial feasts, special days, sacrifices, dietary restrictions, cleansings, etc. The term never applies solely to either the Ten Commandments or the Sabbath.

Realistically speaking, no Seventh-day Adventist *really* keeps "the law." Where are their blood sacrifices? Do they heat their houses on Saturday? They are all law-breakers if they carefully and honestly examine their lives in light of the entire law. The Bible makes no distinction regarding the law, that some parts are "ceremonial" as the Seventh-day Adventists claim—a statement designed to avoid truly keeping the law in its entirety.

The Law Was for the Nation of Israel Only

Regarding the Ten Commandments, Exodus 20:2 states, "I am the Lord your God, who *brought you out of the land of Egypt* out of the house of slavery" (emphasis added). The Ten Commandments were obviously given to those who had been brought out of the land of Egypt. This would limit the Ten Commandments to God's chosen people the Israelites, the Jews.

Deuteronomy 5:3 shows that the law was binding on those Israelites or Jews alive in Moses' day: "The Lord did not make this covenant with our fathers, but with us, with all those of us alive here today." Therefore, no covenant was made with Adam, Noah, Abraham, Isaac, Jacob, Joseph, etc. as claimed by Seventh-day Adventists.

Sabbath-Keeping

Seventh-day Adventists make the Saturday Sabbath of extreme importance in their plan of salvation. Yet it is not commanded for Christians, and Deuteronomy 5:15 applies it only to the Jews:

> And you shall remember that *you were a slave in the land of Egypt*, and the Lord your God brought you out of there by a mighty hand and by an outstretched arm; *therefore* the Lord your God commanded you to *observe the Sabbath day* (emphasis added).

Notice that the Sabbath was a special covenant for those people delivered from bondage in Egypt (see also Ezekiel 20:10-12; Exodus 31:12-18; Exodus 16:29; Nehemiah 9:13, 14).

Is the Sabbath a Memorial of Creation?

It is true that Genesis 2:3 says God blessed the seventh day and sanctified it, but there was no command to memorialize it in remembrance of creation. The command to keep the Sabbath day went only to those who were slaves in Egypt. There is no biblical record of the Sabbath being kept in the interim between creation and the days of Moses. Why? Obviously because it was not commanded to be kept.

I have carefully looked up every Scripture reference given by the Seventh-day Adventists regarding Sabbath-keeping (Genesis 2:1,2; Exodus 20:8-11; Luke 4:16; Isaiah 56:5,6, 58:13,14; Matthew 12:1-12; Exodus 31:13-17; Ezekiel 4:16, 20:12,20; Deuteronomy 5:12-15; Hebrews 4:1-11; Leviticus 23:32; Mark 1:32). All commands to keep the

Sabbath are Old Testament ones to the sons of Israel. The Scripture from Isaiah 56:5,6, has reference to a "memorial *name*," not a *day*. The New Testament references are not commands to keep the Sabbath.

Is the Sabbath "Ceremonial"?

Seventh-day Adventists in particular get out of keeping all the points of the law by claiming some are *"ceremonial"* and don't require strict observance, but in their understanding the Sabbath does require strict observance. Leviticus 23 lists several "holy convocations." The first-mentioned one is the seventh-day Sabbath. The chapter goes on to list other "holy convocations," namely the Passover, the Feast of Unleavened Bread, the wave offering, the Feast of Booths, etc. All are identified as "holy convocations." Why then claim that the first one mentioned, namely the seventh-day Sabbath, is *not* "ceremonial" but *all others* listed are? Let's interpret the Bible honestly and in context, and let's be consistent!

Are Christians Under the Sabbath Law?

Seventh-day Adventists judge Christians very harshly for not keeping "sundown Friday to sundown Saturday." Christians, on the other hand, don't condemn others for worshiping on Saturday if that is their preference. Christians recognize that we are under grace and not under the law. The apostle Paul wrote to the Colossians,

> Therefore let no one act as your judge in regard
> to food or drink or in respect to a festival or a new
> moon or *a Sabbath day*—things which are a

mere shadow of what is to come; but the substance belongs to Christ (Colossians 2:16,17, emphasis added).

No one calling himself a Christian should judge another respecting the Sabbath, and yet the Seventh-day Adventist church would have Christians receive the "mark of the beast" for not keeping the Saturday Sabbath. They have therefore made salvation dependent on which day of the week one keeps.

Hebrews, chapter 4, shows that the fulfillment of the Jewish Sabbath was not the keeping of the same day by Christians, but the entering of Christians into God's rest. The early Christians preached on the Jewish Sabbath because the Jews were gathered in the synagogue on that day. Acts 17:2-4 says,

> And according to Paul's custom, he went to them, and for three Sabbaths reasoned with them from the Scriptures, explaining and giving evidence that the Christ had to suffer and rise again from the dead, and saying, "This Jesus whom I am proclaiming to you is the Christ." And some of them were persuaded and joined Paul and Silas, along with a great multitude of the God-fearing Greeks and a number of the leading women.

Their Christian fellowship together was on the "first day" of the week, Sunday—the day of Christ's resurrection. Acts 20:7 says, "And on the first day of the week, when we were gathered together to break bread, Paul began talking to them, intending to depart the next day, and he prolonged his message until midnight." This was obviously a church meeting, not a witnessing opportunity, and the church still meets on the first day of the week, Sunday.

Conclusions Regarding the Sabbath

There is *no* Scripture commanding Christians to keep the Saturday Sabbath. Surely there would be a command if it was of such importance as to affect our salvation. Christians have always met for fellowship and the breaking of bread on the first day of the week, Sunday, and continue to do so until this day. They do not claim Sunday is the "Sabbath" but rather the "Lord's Day."

Sunday worship was not introduced by the Roman Catholic church, although they like to take credit for it. Catholics merely carried on where the apostles left off. The claim by Seventh-day Adventists that Christians are worshiping the sun by meeting on Sunday is just as ridiculous as Christians accusing the Seventh-day Adventists of worshiping Saturn because they meet on Saturday!

We Are Not Under the Law!

The law was our tutor, or teacher, leading us to Christ. Galatians 3:25 concludes "we are no longer under a tutor." The law divided Jews from Gentiles, so Christ abolished it. Ephesians 2:14-16 says,

> For He Himself is our peace, who made both groups into one, and broke down the barrier of the dividing wall, by abolishing in His flesh the enmity, which is the Law of commandments contained in ordinances, that in Himself He might

make the two into one new man, thus establish-
ing peace, and might reconcile them both in one
body to God through the cross, by it having put to
death the enmity.

Even the Jews knew the Old Law Covenant would pass
away. Jeremiah 31:31 says "'Behold, days are coming,'
declares the Lord, 'when I will make a new covenant with
the house of Israel and with the house of Judah.'"

God would write His new law on people's hearts (v. 33).
Jesus Christ Himself instituted the new covenant (see
1 Corinthians 11:25), fulfilling and abolishing the Old
Law Covenant. Yes, the Old Law Covenant, including the
seventh-day Sabbath observance, is now over. The letter of
the law is finished. Christ Himself is described as the end
(Greek *telos* or "terminator") of the law (Romans 10:4). We
will close this subject by quoting Romans 8:2-4:

For the law of the Spirit of life in Christ Jesus
has set you free from the law of sin and of death.
For what the Law could not do, weak as it was
through the flesh, God did: sending His own Son
in the likeness of sinful flesh and as an offering
for sin, He condemned sin in the flesh, in order
that the requirement of the Law might be fulfilled in us, who do not walk according to the
flesh, but according to the Spirit.

The 1844 Investigative Judgment Doctrine

The investigative judgment doctrine, peculiar to Seventh-
day Adventists, teaches that in fulfillment of Old Testament sanctuary typology, Christ entered into the second
apartment of the sanctuary in heaven in 1844 in order to

begin a work of "investigative judgment" to see who was worthy of eternal life, both of those still living and those dead.

A brief background for this teaching is called for. Ellen G. White, under the influence of William Miller, an early Adventist, agreed with his date for the visible return of Christ. October 1844 was set for the second coming of Christ. Christ obviously did not return on that date, so in order to "save face" over a false prophecy, "investigative judgment" was born. In Seventh-day Adventist theology 1844 came to be the date when a work of final atonement which would blot out a believer's sin would begin.

This teaching is the opposite of the full atonement taught by the Christian church, and also mocks at the words of our Savior from the cross, "It is finished" (John 19:30). Hebrews 10:12 states, "But He, having offered one sacrifice for sins, for all time, sat down at the right hand of God."

Christ paid fully for our sins, atoning for them fully. No Scripture teaches otherwise.

Serious Ramifications of the 1844 Investigative Judgment Teaching

In 1877 Uriah Smith, an early Adventist, declared, "Christ did not make the atonement when he shed his blood upon the cross. Let this fact be fixed forever in the mind" (*The Sanctuary and the Twenty-Three Hundred Days of Daniel VIII, 14*, p. 276, quoted in *Are the Gospel and the 1844 Theology Compatible?* by Robert D. Brinsmead, p. 17).

Ellen White herself declared (or plagiarized) in *The Great Controversy* that "before Christ's work for the redemption of men is completed, there is a work of atonement for the removal of sin from the sanctuary. This is the service which began when the 2300 days ended" (1844).

We will not be citing page numbers for *The Great Controversy* since so many editions were printed, but by looking in the index for the subject, the quotes can be found. So Ellen White places the time of Christ's atonement after 1844.

While plagiarizing various evangelical writers of this time, she did also copy statements teaching that redemption was finished at the cross, and some Seventh-day Adventists like to quote only these references. But in all honesty, they must admit the Seventh-day Adventist view was and is a denial of the atoning work of Christ at Calvary.

There is even found in *The Great Controversy* this denial of Him as our absolute mediator:

> Those who are living upon the earth when the intercession of Christ shall cease in the sanctuary above, are to stand in the sight of a holy God without a mediator. Their robes must be spotless, their characters must be purified from sin by the blood of sprinkling. Through the grace of God and their own diligent effort, they must be conquerors in the battle with evil.

Later in the same book this statement is made, "In that fearful time the righteous must live in the sight of a holy God without an intercessor." What a terrible thought to have to stand before God without Christ as our mediator! Thank God for the assurance found in 1 John 2:1: "And if anyone sins, we have an Advocate [intercessor] with the Father, Jesus Christ the righteous."

Who Bears Our Sins?

The answer to the above question comes quickly to the Christian because the Scriptures plainly teach that Christ "bore our sins *in His body* on the cross" (1 Peter 2:24, emphasis added). Second Corinthians 5:21 says that Christ was "made ... to be sin on our behalf."

The Seventh-day Adventists go one step further and say that Christ will in turn lay our sins on Satan, who will bear them! Their strange interpretation of Leviticus 16—making Satan the scapegoat—is unsupported by Christian theologians, and is further proof that by using *The Great Controversy* as their guide, Seventh-day Adventists would add to Christ's finished work of atonement.

The Denial of Hell and the Doctrine of Soul-Sleep

In the early 1800s, groups began arising that taught that hell was not a place of eternal torment. "Soul-sleep," or a state of unconsciousness, replaced torment. Seventh-day Adventists embraced this doctrine, but is this view correct according to the Bible?

Three Words for Hell

Most of the confusion surrounding the topic of hell is because the King James Version of the Bible translated three distinct Greek words by the one word "hell." The three Greek words are *tartaros, hades,* and *Gehenna.* Only one of these three words refers to the place of eternal torment commonly called "hell," and the other words are often given mistaken meanings. Let's consider these three words and their meanings.

Tartaros (Hell)

Tartaros need not concern us too much since it is a special abode for angels who are confined to this special pit of darkness. The word *Tartaros* occurs only once in the New Testament, in 2 Peter 2:4.

Hades (Hell)

Hades, also translated "hell" occurs ten times in the New Testament and is referred to by three writers: Matthew, Luke, and John. The most detailed information we can find about Hades is in Luke 16 where we are told about a rich man and Lazarus. Lazarus died in a righteous condition and the angels took him into Abraham's bosom, to a place of peace and security. The rich man, on the other hand, went to *Hades* or *hell* and was in great torment. He was obviously fully conscious of his surroundings and not in a condition of so-called "soul-sleep," for the account in Luke records, "The rich man also died, and was buried. And in Hades he lifted up his eyes, being in torment" (Luke 16:22,23).

He pleaded for a drop of water to cool his tongue because of the torment of the flame. He could also see the happy condition of Lazarus, but could not leave his place of torment. He spoke about his worry over his five brothers who had yet to die. He wished to spare them his present agony. Yes, this pitiful rich man had all his faculties and was indeed experiencing ongoing torment.

Is Luke 16 only a parable? Groups like the Jehovah's Witnesses and Seventh-day Adventists who deny the reality of hellfire do indeed claim that the above account is "only a parable" or is "figurative" or "spiritual." However this account is not a parable since proper names of recognizable Bible characters are used, whereas Jesus never used proper names in His parables and generally indicated when He was teaching in a parable. Even stretching the point and allowing that Luke 16 could be a parable, it teaches a spiritual truth, and Jesus taught truth, not falsehoods.

Hades in the Greek finds its parallel in the Hebrew word *Sheol*. Hades and Sheol (both translated "hell"), are often called "holding tanks" by some Bible scholars since souls in this "hell" are not in their final destination. According to Revelation 20, those in Hades will yet face the great white throne judgment. Hades will be terminated at this time. Those with condemnatory judgment will be cast into *Gehenna* (hell), the "lake that burns with Fire and Sulphur."

Gehenna (Hell)—The Final Destination

The term *Gehenna*, also translated "hell," occurs 12 times in the New Testament, and every quote is by Jesus Christ. Six of the 12 references to *Gehenna* mention fire as one of its characteristics.

Southeast of Jerusalem was the Valley of the Son of Hinnom. During Old Testament times, children were offered to the false god Moloch in this valley, and later Jews used this valley to dispose of their rubbish, as well as the bodies of dead animals and unburied criminals. To consume all this, a fire was kept burning continuously, and gnawing worms abounded. It was a vile place. The Jews of Jesus' day certainly had a vivid picture of what being thrown alive into *Gehenna* would mean for them.

What Did Jesus Say About Gehenna?

We have only to read the words of Jesus in Mark 9:42-48 to know the seriousness of a destination of *Gehenna*:

> And whosoever shall offend one of these little
> ones that believe in me, it is better for him that a
> millstone were hanged about his neck, and he
> were cast into the sea. And if thy hand offend
> thee, cut if off; it is better for thee to enter into
> life maimed, then having two hands to go into
> hell [or *Gehenna*], into the fire that never shall
> be quenched: where their worm dieth not, and
> the fire is not quenched (KJV).

The same warning is issued regarding a foot or an eye
that would hinder us, that "the fire would not be quenched,"
and "their worm would not die." Christ stressed that it
would be better to lose the most precious things in this life
and avoid hell than to retain all that this life holds dear
and be cast into this dreadful place. Why all these warn-
ings by the Lord Himself if we are only going to be unconscious?

What About "Soul-Sleep"?

A condition of soul-sleep is obviously not taught by
Christ. The inhabitants of hell are not unconscious or
annihilated. When we really believe the Word of God as it
is written and don't try to "figuratize" or "spiritualize" it
away, it becomes evident that hell is a very real destination, and its inhabitants are conscious.

Let's compare Revelation 19:20 with Revelation 20:10.
Notice that before the 1000-year reign of Christ the beast
and the false prophet were cast into the lake of fire. Were
they annihilated in that lake of fire (hell)? No, for 1000
years later they are still alive, and the devil joins them in
their condition of torment. Scripture says plainly, "They
will be tormented day and night forever and ever."

Two Destinations

Let's believe the words of Jesus Christ in Matthew 25:46 that there are two destinations: one for believers and one for unbelievers. "And these will go away into eternal punishment, but the righteous into eternal life." The same exact word in the Greek describes both conditions. Both are "everlasting," "eternal," and "ongoing." We may choose eternal life, or eternal punishment and torment. Denying the reality of hell won't prevent us from going there! Seventh-day Adventists need to reconsider their doctrine on hellfire in light of the Scriptures alone.

Trusting in Ellen G. White

Seventh-day Adventism rises or falls on Ellen G. White, since the modern Seventh-day Adventist church continues to endorse her and her doctrines. I do not need to elaborate on the excellent research already done by her former followers, proving that she plagiarized almost all of her writings, even while claiming "visions" from God.

After a decade and a half in the cults ministry, we can state for a fact that our most angry, hateful mail comes from Seventh-day Adventists. Most of them rail against us anonymously, which does not afford us an opportunity to reply with the truth of the matter and give them references to check out in their own publications.

Nevertheless, we had hopes that following the shake-up caused by the exposé of their prophetess and the White Estate, the Seventh-day Adventist church would renounce her doctrines and move into the evangelical Christian group. However, we have allowed ample time for this to happen. Instead, the Seventh-day Adventist church has chosen its prophetess and her organization.

Therefore we believe that it is a cult for the following reasons:

1. Misrepresentation of Jesus Christ as to His person, mediatorship, and atoning work.

2. Due to its claim to exclusivity. Seventh-day Adventists believe they alone will receive salvation, avoiding the "mark of the beast." They believe they alone are the "remnant church."

3. Salvation has been "boiled down" to which day of the week you keep. Grace has been contaminated with extreme legalism and works.

4. Because Seventh-day Adventists choose to endorse a proven false prophetess and embrace her teachings, even after the truth was shown to the leaders.

Seventh-day Adventists still like to point out that the late Dr. Walter Martin, a cult expert, did not regard them as a cult in his book, *Kingdom of the Cults*. However, on public television during "The John Ankerberg Show" he made this statement:

I fear that if they continue to progress at this rate, then the classification of a cult can't possibly miss being reapplied to Seventh-day Adventism, because once you have an interpreter of Scripture, a final court of appeal that tells you what Scripture means, as soon as you judge Scripture by that, as soon as you have someone who has made doctrinal errors in the past, even on the deity of Christ and the doctrine of the atonement and other things, and that person is raised to that position or authority, you have polarization around that person.

Sadly, Seventh-day Adventism has missed its opportunity to align its doctrines with the Bible alone and join with evangelical Christianity. By its own actions of late, it has placed itself in the category of a cult. We can now only hope for future changes.

Chapter 5

THE CHANGING WORLDWIDE CHURCH OF GOD

The original Worldwide Church of God was founded by Herbert W. Armstrong. He died at 93 years of age on January 16, 1986, leaving 80,000 members and his "World Tomorrow" broadcast on 374 TV stations and 30 radio stations. His successor is Joseph W. Tkach, but the Worldwide Church of God is no longer a "one-man show," and a variety of speakers now appear on the telecasts. The church is in a state of flux, presently altering some of Herbert W. Armstrong's favorite doctrines and upsetting many longtime members.

The ego of founder Herbert W. Armstrong is legendary. He alone claimed to have restored the true gospel (which was supposedly lost) in 1934. *The Plain Truth* magazine had this statement in the July/August 1973 issue: "The work going on from Ambassador College and the Worldwide Church of God, is the ONLY WORK ON EARTH proclaiming the very gospel of Jesus Christ to the world in great power."

The Plain Truth magazine of February 1958 on page 23 proclaims, "Yes, this work is the work of the true Church of God. All others are satanic counterfeits!"

Many Worldwide Church of God members are disturbed that Herbert W. Armstrong's most powerful doctrinal books are now "out of print," namely, *Mystery of the Ages, The Incredible Human Potential, The Wonderful World Tomorrow, Book of Revelation Unveiled at Last,* and *H.W.A.'s Autobiography, Volume 1,* to name a few. *The United States and Britain in Prophecy* is under review and reportedly drastically reduced, and many of H.W. Armstrong's articles and booklets have been rewritten, altering the original message.

The Peculiar Doctrines of the Worldwide Church of God

The Worldwide Church of God was marked by its emphasis on prophecy when Herbert W. Armstrong was its chief prophet. Since Jesus repeatedly warned us against believing false prophets in Matthew 24, we need to examine the past prophecies of this group.

In 1956 a booklet now "out of print" was published titled *1975 in Prophecy!* which readers were urged to read twice so it would be "twice as REAL!" The booklet foretold a major drought for the United States of America by no later than 1975. This did not happen.

The Plain Truth, the official magazine of the Worldwide Church of God, produced a large headline in February 1956, proclaiming, "U.S.A. RIDING TO TOTAL COLLAPSE IN 20 SHORT YEARS!" The United States did not collapse in 1976, nor did Americans and British find themselves enslaved as Herbert W. Armstrong prophesied.

Armstrong promised deliverance by an exodus for his people from these foretold troubles. The place of supposed safety was called "Petra" and was located in Jordan. People were urged to sell their homes and contribute money to a

"Petra Fund." Those who refused to contribute to the Petra Fund were threatened with going into the "Laodicean" church group, which was consigned to the great tribulation.

As late as spring 1970, Herbert Armstrong announced that he was still 95 percent sure that the United States would go into captivity in January 1972. As one follower remembers, "We would flee to the place of safety and be protected for three-and-one-half years from the beast power." Followers with longer memories would recall that final destruction was first slated for 1938.

A Faulty Foundation

Although the present leadership has taken this false prophecy and others out of print, if the foundation is faulty, the whole organization is faulty since it is based on the teachings of a false prophet. Could Herbert W. Armstrong be so wrong on his prophecies and yet be right on his doctrines? Let's investigate further.

Salvation Delayed

In the gospel of the Worldwide Church of God founded by Herbert W. Armstrong, you could not be "born-again" or "saved" until your resurrection! In his booklet *Just What Do You Mean—Born Again?* Armstrong pointed out,

> We do not enter into and inherit the Kingdom of God while still flesh and blood, but only after the resurrection to *spirit composition*. Being born again refers to the time—the future state— when we shall *be* spirit, no longer flesh and blood—born actually by the resurrection. The

experience of conversion, in this life, is a begettal—
a "conception"—an "impregnation"—but *not yet
a birth* (emphasis added).

In Herbert W. Armstrong's day, Worldwide Church of
God followers, when converted, apparently lived out their
lives as "embryos" but were finally "born again" at their
death and resurrection.

Now, however, Pastor General Joseph Tkach, in the
January 28, 1991 issue of *The Worldwide News*, reported
that Worldwide Church of God members are already "born
again." This is a direct contradiction of their founder's
teachings. We find the following amazing statements in
the article on page 6:

> It is a correct biblical analogy to refer to the
> Christian as having been born again.... It is
> referring to conversion.... In summary, we must
> understand that when the Bible speaks of a per-
> son as being "born again," it is speaking of the
> Christian conversion, not of the ultimate Chris-
> tian inheritance.

Herbert W. Armstrong's doctrine on being "born again"
at the time of the resurrection was dismissed as his "mis-
understanding" the Greek.

Salvation in the Worldwide Church of God

Some researchers have assumed in the past that Herbert W. Armstrong taught salvation by "works." However,
we have found that he did teach salvation by grace alone,
at least initially. To explain his view, when one accepted

the free gift of salvation he was forgiven of all *past* sins only. Herbert W. Armstrong taught that from that point on, there were conditions, namely continuing obedience to authority to keep the person in a state of being justified.

Currently, Tkach seems to be teaching much the same thing, but we are watching for changes. After all, most cult groups must keep their members continually striving, working, and in fear of judgment in order to keep control. Whatever changes come, we still expect to see lots of "works" required by the Worldwide Church of God hierarchy.

Jesus, on the other hand told His followers to *hear* and *believe.* John 5:24 says, "Truly, truly, I say to you, he who hears My word, and believes Him who sent Me, has eternal life, and does not come into judgment, but has passed out of death into life."

Make no mistake about it, however: If one is truly born again or saved, he will have works in his life. These works will be the fruits of his salvation experience. He will not do works under compulsion or unwillingly, but he will not be able to stop the outpouring of the love felt in his heart for his Savior. Works are a *result* of salvation, not a *condition* for remaining justified as the Worldwide Church of God teaches to this day. However, we are pleased to see the Worldwide Church of God moving toward a more biblical view of matters and hope the trend will continue.

The Trinity Versus the Family of God

While recent developments in the Worldwide Church of God indicate they are revising their non-Trinitarian view of God, even viewing Trinitarians as being honest in their attempt to explain God, to date nothing official has changed so we will review their present doctrine.

The Plain Truth magazine of February 1960 on page 26 contained this statement: "The true teaching of the Bible is that the Father and Son comprise the One Kingdom or Family of God. The Holy Spirit is the common nature, mind, and force of God."

The Worldwide Church of God in the past has relegated the Trinity to paganism, taken away the deity of the Holy Spirit, and changed the triune God into a family. This was done to allow for the doctrine that each follower could be God.

Page 21 of the booklet *Why Were You Born?* said, "At the time of the resurrection we shall be instantaneously CHANGED from mortal into immortal—we shall then be *born* of God—*we shall then be God!*" (emphasis added).

Not only did Worldwide Church of God publications discuss subjects like "What it means to be equal with God" (*Tomorrow's World*, April, 1971), but on page 45 the same article went on to promise Worldwide Church of God followers that they would someday advise and counsel God Himself!

The Worldwide Church of God appears to be backing down now on the teaching that they will be God someday. We welcome this direction in their thinking and wish to point out that Revelation 5:10 promises Christians that they will be joint heirs with Christ as kings and priests. Kings and priests, yes! God, never! God Almighty has an exclusive claim on "Godship." Isaiah 45:22 declares, "I am God, and there is none else" (KJV). Isaiah 48:11 says, "And I will not give my glory unto another" (KJV).

God is always the Creator, and we are always the creatures, and this continues for all eternity. Revelation 4 shows the Father and Son being worshiped by all others. They alone are worshiped. We will never be God or gods, and to teach this doctrine is Hinduism, New Age, or Mormonism, but it is not Christianity!

The Doctrine of the Triple Tithe

Many interested persons are impressed that all literature from the Worldwide Church of God is offered free and donations are sometimes not accepted if sent. On the surface it seems like a refreshing break from the usual TV gospel. Just wait until you join! You will be expected to triple tithe. After all, how do you think they pay for all the freebies?

Followers of the Worldwide Church of God must pay 10 percent of their gross income to the church. In addition they are to set aside another 10 percent to attend conventions such as the Feast of Tabernacles. They are expected to tithe 10 percent of this second tithe for festival expenses, and use the rest to attend the festivals themselves. On top of this, every third and sixth year in a cycle of seven years they must pay to the church another 10 percent of gross income, which is supposed to be used for needy ones within the movement. There have been serious problems in past years over church misuse of this third tithe. One thing is certain: The Worldwide Church of God is wealthy due to its tithing members.

The Keeping of the Seventh-day Sabbath and the Law

On page 58 of H.W. Armstrong's booklet *Which Day Is the Christian Sabbath?* he marks the keeping of sundown Friday to sundown Saturday as a sign identifying the true Christians today. He says the Sabbath command is "the one on which YOUR VERY SALVATION and ETERNITY

DEPENDS!" His followers had to also keep seven Old Testament festivals as well. This practice continues today.

We have done an extensive work of replying to these doctrines on the Sabbath and keeping of the law in the chapter on Seventh-day Adventism, which shares common views with the Worldwide Church of God, so please refer to chapter 4 for a biblical response to the claim that Christians must keep the Old Law Sabbath. Christians are not under the law.

The Rejection of Christmas and Easter

The Worldwide Church of God attacks the observance of Christmas and Easter, charging that they are pagan practices and not for Christians. No one can deny that these observances have been abused by those in the world, but should this stop Christians from observing them in a proper manner?

The Date December 25 and Its Origin

First off, we can all agree that we do not know the exact date of Christ's birth. Secondly, we can all agree that pagans celebrate on this date. We would be hard-pressed to find a day to celebrate that did not have pagan roots. Every day of our week—indeed our entire calendar—is pagan! However, all would agree that these pagan roots have lost their significance. Do Worldwide Church of God members when observing their Sabbath refuse to observe it because it is held on a day that once involved the worship of Saturn? Likewise, Christians do not refuse to honor Jesus just because of pagan roots, since these pagan roots have no significance to them. Why then choose December 25 to celebrate Christ's birth?

In the *Israel My Glory* magazine of December/January 1986/87 there appeared an article called "Why Do We Celebrate Christmas on December 25th?" Since Christianity has its roots in Judaism and not in paganism, let's look to the Jewish roots for the origin of our date, as did this article.

A full explanation of the Jewish observance of Chanukkah (also called Hanukkah) is given since it is a major holiday for Jews to this day. Although it was not one of the seven biblical holidays, it nevertheless is of great significance. It is also called "The Festival of Dedication," or sometimes "The Festival of Lights." John 10:22,23 records that Jesus was walking on the porch of the temple during this observance. He had nothing to say against it and, judging by His location, may have been participating, even though attendance was not explicitly commanded in the Bible.

On page 5, this article says,

> December 25th is almost certainly not the actual date for the incarnation. Shepherds in Israel would not have been out in the fields tending their flocks at night in December. Therefore, why choose this date? First, it was on the 25th day of the Hebrew month Kislev (corresponding to our December) that Antiochus chose to desecrate the Temple and establish worship of his god because it was already an existing heathen holiday. Therefore, 1 and 2 Maccabees go out of their way to stress the fact that it was exactly three years later, to the day, that the Temple was cleansed and rededicated (the 25th of Kislev).
>
> Now when the Church, long after the actual date of the incarnation had been lost in antiquity, chose the date to commemorate the incomparable occasion when

deity dwelt within a human body, what better association than the Temple, where deity had also dwelt, and the 25th of Kislev, which was an already established date commemorating the cleansing and rededication of the Temple as a dwelling place for God?

The Church did not choose December 25th because it was an ancient heathen holiday, but because of the Jewish feast of Chanukkah that occurred on that date, and the added significance that Jesus gave to it. This date eloquently testified to the fact that at the birth of Jesus deity was dwelling in a human body (Temple) and shining out to give light in the midst of darkness. The great Hebrew-Christian scholar, Alfred Edersheim, whose writings on this period of time are still classic, shared this thought, "The date of the feast of Dedication (Chanukkah)—the 25th of Kislev—seems to have been adopted by the ancient church as that of the birth of our blessed Lord—Christmas—the dedication of the true temple which was the body of Jesus."

The Worldwide Church of God which is usually attracted to anything "Jewish" would do well to look at the Jewish roots of our Christmas (which means "Christ is sent") and act accordingly.

The Origin of the Christmas Tree

Our custom of the lighted Christmas tree originated with Martin Luther, a great man of God. While walking in the moonlight and thanking God for sending His Son, he saw an evergreen tree covered in hoarfrost shining in the moonlight. He cut the tree down and brought it inside and decorated its branches with lit candles to remind all that Christ is the light of the world. The tree is symbolic of the "tree of life" referred to in Revelation. The feeble attempt of some cults to link the Christmas tree with Jeremiah, chapter 10, is cleared up when we read it in context. Here a woodcutter takes a tree, carves it into an idol, and worships it. The Christmas tree has never been worshiped yet in a Christian home!

Since God saw fit to have the angels sing and rejoice at the birth of Christ (Luke 2:13,14), and we are commanded to "honor the Son even as [we] honor the Father" (John 5:23), we make no apology to the cults for celebrating the birth of our Savior, Christ the Lord, on whatever day we choose.

Easter and Its Meaning to Christians

Once again, as with Christmas, Christians are confronted with paganism connected with their Christian celebration of the resurrection of Christ. Just because the name "Easter," which has come into common usage, has pagan roots, should Christians cease to celebrate the resurrection of their Savior? Of course not. Let the world have its bunnies and eggs on the same day if they wish. It should not interfere with our joy in the risen Christ.

The Wrong View of the Resurrection

The Worldwide Church of God denies the bodily resurrection of Jesus Christ, teaching that He was raised "a spirit." First Peter 3:18 is used, which says Jesus was "made alive in the spirit" to support their doctrine that

Jesus rose "a spirit." However, the term "in the spirit" does not mean "a spirit."

The apostle John was "in the Spirit" in Revelation 1:10. Are we to assume that John lost his body and became "a spirit"? Hardly. Romans 8:9 tells us that the whole congregation was "in the Spirit." Does this likewise mean that the whole congregation lost their bodies and became spirits? No, of course not.

Jesus was made alive in the power of the Holy Spirit. Romans 8:11 says this: "But if the Spirit of Him who raised Jesus from the dead dwells in you, He who raised Christ Jesus from the dead will also give life to your mortal bodies through His Spirit who indwells you."

The account in Luke, chapter 24, is devastating to the Worldwide Church of God doctrine on the resurrection. In this account, Jesus Himself appeared in the midst of His believers. Verse 37 records, "But they were startled and frightened and thought that they were seeing a spirit" (Worldwide Church of God doctrine exactly!).

Jesus said to them in verse 39, "See My hands and My feet, that it is *I Myself*; touch Me and see, for *a spirit does not have flesh and bones* as you see that *I have*" (emphasis added). Jesus Christ was not raised "a spirit" but had a *bodily* resurrection. John 2:19-21 says,

> Jesus answered and said to them, "Destroy this temple, and in three days I will raise it up." The Jews therefore said, "It took forty-six years to build this temple, and will You raise it up in three days?" But He was speaking of the temple of His body.

The Worldwide Church of God admits it has its own definition for the word "resurrection." They have redefined the word to mean "re-creation," as do the Jehovah's Witnesses, both in order to teach their faulty doctrine of "soul-sleep" or nonexistence after death. The Bible does not teach either "soul-sleep" or "re-creation," but teaches true resurrection—dying and rising again. It's simple, but of prime importance to believe that Christ died and rose again, and we live because He lives.

What Day Did Christ Rise?

Armstrong wrote a booklet called *The Resurrection Was Not on Sunday.* We would like to biblically refute that error. Mark records that the women reached the tomb of Jesus just as the sun was beginning to rise on the first day of the week (Mark 16:1,2). Luke and John also record this (Luke 24:1; John 20:1). In Luke, chapter 24, we first have the account of the women arriving at the tomb "on the first day of the week." Later in this same chapter Luke records that two disciples were on the Emmaus road on this same first day of the week. Listen to their remark: "It is the third day since these things happened" (Luke 24:21). The risen Christ was walking with them and revealed Himself. Jesus Himself said He would rise on the "third day" in Luke 18:33 and that "third day" was the "first day of the week," namely Sunday. Thereafter the Bible records believers meeting on "the first day of the week" for worship and the breaking of bread (Acts 20:7).

Therefore it is right and proper to keep Resurrection Sunday, also called Easter Sunday, as well as to meet for worship and communion on Sunday. The dispute now comes down to which day of the week Christ died. The church traditionally says Friday. However, some scholars do agree with Armstrong that it might have been earlier in the week.

What About the "Sign" and the "Three Days and Three Nights Controversy"?

The Plain Truth magazine of March 1966, page 30, stated, "Jesus gave only one sign to prove that He was the Messiah. That sign was the length of time He would be dead and buried." Matthew 12:40 is then quoted which states, "So shall the Son of man be three days and three nights in the heart of the earth." The emphasis on the length of time between the time of Jesus' burial and resurrection is a clever way of covering up their gross error made in the manner of Christ's resurrection. Christ had a bodily resurrection (John 2:19-21). He was not raised a spirit as Armstrong taught (Luke 24:39-42).

We agree that Matthew 12:40 says, "For just as Jonah was three days and three nights in the belly of the sea monster, so shall the Son of Man be three days and three nights in the heart of the earth."

We should expect literal fulfillment of this prophecy, for the Bible is true. However, with the current teaching that the crucifixion was on "Good Friday" and the resurrection on Sunday, we are all hard-pressed to come up with three full days and three full nights for Jesus to be in the "heart of the earth." We have already shown from the Bible that Jesus definitely rose on Sunday. We must count back from that established point.

Mark 15:42 says the crucifixion took place on "the preparation day, that is, the day before the Sabbath." The regular weekly Jewish Sabbath being Saturday would therefore make this reference seem to refer to Friday.

However, Jews also called other "feast days" or "high days" by the term "Sabbath." These "feast day Sabbaths" could fall on any day of the week. John 19:31 identifies the

Sabbath at the time of Jesus' crucifixion as a "high day Sabbath":

> The Jews therefore, because it was the day of preparation, so that the bodies should not remain on the cross on the Sabbath (for that Sabbath was a high day), asked Pilate that their legs might be broken, and that they might be taken away.

So possibly there were two Sabbaths during the week of Jesus' crucifixion: a "high Sabbath" and a regular weekly Sabbath. This could allow for a day other than Friday being the day of Jesus' crucifixion.

Why place such importance on the actual day of Jesus' death? The important thing is not *when* Christ died, but *why* Christ died. The most important reason to celebrate is that He *rose again*, defeating death, and we live because He lives. We keep Sunday—"resurrection day"—for this very reason.

The Theory of British Israelism

At time of printing we are awaiting expected changes to the British Israelism theory introduced by the Late Herbert W. Armstrong. We anticipate that this doctrine may be dropped entirely, but it is still of interest as it affects the history of the Worldwide Church of God.

The theory taught that when God's people returned to Palestine after the captivity, only the tribes of Judah, Benjamin, and Levi really returned. The "House of Israel," meaning the ten lost tribes, scattered. By Jesus' day, supposedly only three tribes were represented. According to the theory, the "House of Israel" was missing.

The apostle Peter was, however, unaware of Mr. Armstrong's teaching that the house of Israel was supposed to be missing, since he uttered these words at Acts 2:36, "Therefore let all the house of Israel know for certain that God has made Him both Lord and Christ—this Jesus whom you crucified."

Are "Israel" and "Jew" Always Different?

Armstrong taught that the terms "Israel" and "Jew" meant two separate nations. In his interpretation, "Jew" in its national reference always meant "the house of Judah," and "Israel" likewise meant "the lost ten tribes." Second Kings 17:18-23 is a favorite passage of British-Israelism devotees, so let's consider it:

> So the LORD was very angry with Israel, and removed them from His sight, none was left except the tribe of Judah. Also Judah did not keep the commandments of the Lord their God, but walked in the customs which Israel had introduced. And the Lord rejected all the descendants of Israel and afflicted them and gave them into the hand of plunderers, until He had cast them out of His sight. When He had torn Israel from the house of David, they made Jeroboam the son of Nebat king. Then Jeroboam drove Israel away from following the Lord, and made them commit a great sin. And the sons of Israel walked in all the sins of Jeroboam which he did; they did not depart from them, until the Lord removed Israel from His sight, as He spoke

through all His servants the prophets. So Israel
was carried away into exile from their own land
to Assyria until this day.

Notice the last phrase of this Scripture. Israel went as
far as Assyria unto this day. They relocated, but not far
away—certainly not across oceans!

The Rebuilding of Jerusalem in Nehemiah's Day

According to the British-Israelism theory, only Jews
should have been participating in rebuilding Jerusalem
since the house of Israel was "long gone." Yet Ezra uses the
words "all Israel" several times in the account (Ezra 2:70;
6:17; 8:25,35; 10:5; Nehemiah 7:73; 12:47). Evidently the
terms "Jew" and "Israel" were used interchangeably, thus
spoiling Herbert W. Armstrong's theory.

The Ten Tribes in Christ's Day

If the ten tribes were gone by Christ's day, how does
Armstrong explain that Anna the prophetess was of the
tribe of Asher? (Luke 2:36). Paul mentioned all 12 tribes
(Acts 26:6,7). James mentioned all 12 tribes (James 1:1).

The book of Revelation tells of 12,000 people from each of
the 12 tribes of Israel (Revelation 7:4-8). All Israel shall be
saved eventually (Romans 11:26). Upon consulting a Jewish rabbi, he assured me the list in Revelation was a literal
one, as are the other lists in the Bible, although they differ
from one another for various reasons. The Revelation list is
not "figurative" or "spiritual" allowing for interpretation
to apply to some other nation, but applies to literal Israel.

The apostle Paul was addressed in three ways: first, as a Hebrew (Philippians 3:5); secondly, as an Israelite (2 Corinthians 11:22); and thirdly, as a Jew (Acts 21:39; 22:3). Obviously, Paul recognized no such distinctions as invented by this theory. All terms interchange.

Christ the King

Since Christ had a sign over His head on the cross reading "King of the Jews," are we to assume that He was king for Judah only? No, for the Scriptures are plain that Christ was the promised Messiah for all Israel. The disciples understood this when they questioned Him in Acts 1:6: "Lord, is it as this time You are restoring the kingdom to Israel?" Obviously, "Jew" and "Israel" were used interchangeably in Christ's day.

After putting up the sign "King of the Jews," His mockers then said, "He is the King of Israel, Let Him now come down from the cross, and we shall believe in Him" (Matthew 27:42). Again, the terms interchange.

Problems with the Stone

British-Israelism claims that the stone under the Queen of England's coronation chair is the very "pillar stone of Jacob" which was first transported by Jacob and finally by Jeremiah to the British Isles via Egypt. The Scriptures know nothing of this invented event. We would expect, if the theory is correct, that the English coronation stone could be analyzed and found to be of the type found in Israel. The stone has been analyzed and *The Marson Report*, page 128, records, "The stone in Westminster Abbey has been analyzed and shown to be a calcareous type of red sandstone of Scottish origin."

Conclusions on British-Israelism

British-Israelism is not a revelation from God as Herbert W. Armstrong taught. Rather it is a theory that cannot stand up to biblical or scientific examination. It should be rejected by those professing Christianity. We suggest the Worldwide Church of God reject it also.

The Church Goes On

Under the leadership of Joseph W. Tkach the church continues. They have kept as their legacy the lingering influence of Herbert W. Armstrong. We welcome some of the changes we see developing, but we also hear regularly from hurting members who have had their lives and families destroyed by mind control, absolute obedience to harsh authority, and financial hardships. We look for many more changes before we can consider the Worldwide Church of God as anything but a cult.

Chapter 6

THE COMMUNAL CULTS

T oday, with the breakdown of the traditional family, we see arising an alternate "family"—the communal cult. Here, mainly young people find a real sense of "belonging," "parental authority figures," and many "brothers and sisters." Older people who feel a sense of frustration with their jobs or are in mid-life crisis are also candidates for a commune, with its alternate life-style.

Recruiting into Communal Cults

The cult recruiter is to be found on the streets and at the universities. He will generally strike up a conversation with a potential recruit. The encounter is evidently sincere and friendly, and a genuine interest in the recruit is shown. The real nature of the group recruiting is carefully hidden. The deception involved does not bother the recruiter at all and may, in fact, form part of the cult's doctrine. An example is the "heavenly deception" doctrine of the Unification Church (the Moonies), who are careful not to reveal the real name of their group when recruiting or selling items.

The new recruit is continually shown attention and love

and is rarely left alone. By this time the recruit is usually "in residence" at a cult house or commune and finds it increasingly difficult to relate to the outside world. Diet and lack of sleep further cloud the recruit's mind, and intense indoctrination "programs his brain."

Soon, the "love-bombed" new member is ready, willing, and able to serve his new master, isolate himself from his real family, and find continued acceptance among his new "family."

The Unification Church
(The Moonies)

The founder, Sun Myung Moon, was born in Korea in 1920. He authored a book called *Divine Principle*, in which he stated on page 9 that the Bible is "not the truth itself, but a textbook teaching the truth," it must not be regarded as "absolute in every detail." So we find Mr. Moon giving lip service to the Bible but taking tremendous liberties in its interpretation.

Moon's Biblical Interpretations

Consider the events in the Garden of Eden. Mr. Moon teaches that Satan tempted Eve, and then proceeded to have sex relations with her. This, in turn, produced the child Cain who, because of his evil father the devil, started communism. Eve then thought better of the affair, turned to Adam, became his wife, and produced the child Abel— the forefather of democracy.

The Bible plainly identifies Adam as the father of both Cain and Abel. Genesis 4:1,2 says,

> Now the man had relations with his wife Eve,
> and she conceived and gave birth to Cain, and

she said "I have gotten a manchild with the help of the Lord." And again, she gave birth to his brother Abel.

Misrepresentation of Jesus Christ

Mr. Moon teaches that Jesus was just a man who attained deity by fulfilling the purpose of creation, but can by no means be considered to be God Himself (*Divine Principle*, pp. 209-10). Robbing Jesus of His true deity, Mr. Moon then proceeds to brand Jesus Christ a failure. In this same *Divine Principle*, Mr. Moon teaches that Jesus failed in His Christly mission. Mr. Moon goes on to say that Jesus' death on the cross was not an essential part of God's plan for redeeming sinful man. Hebrews 5:9 calls Christ, "the source of eternal salvation." The Bible teaches that Christ died obediently and perfectly, completely paying the penalty for sinful man.

Visitations from the Beyond

Mr. Moon claims to have had visitations from Jesus, Moses, and spirit beings from the netherworld. He claims that Jesus begged him many times to take upon himself the task of redeeming the world. Romans 3:23,24 says clearly that Jesus has already done that: "For all have sinned and fall short of the glory of God, being justified as a gift by His grace through the redemption which is in Christ Jesus."

Watch Out for These Names

The Unification Church presently uses these names, along with others too numerous to list: the Holy Spirit

Association, Holy Spirit Association for the Unification of World Christianity, the United Family, International One World Crusade, CARP, CAUSA, and Interfaith Endeavor. Many times Christians have unwittingly become involved in what they believed to be an interfaith group but turned out to be a front for the Unification Church.

The Unification Church is now active in many businesses and continues to amass wealth. Many people are involved in this far-flung empire without the knowledge that they are part of Mr. Moon's religious empire. Those who do know more often than not won't admit it, hiding behind various names. Christians, be careful to investigate fully any group looking to recruit you and sounding very idealistic. It could be the Moonies.

The Emissaries of Divine Light
(Ontologists)

The Emissaries of Divine Light are a communal group originally founded by Lloyd Meeker in 1945 in Colorado. He assigned himself the title of "bishop" and succeeded in converting Lord Martin Cecil to his beliefs. Meeker died in 1954, and Lord Martin Cecil took over the commune in British Columbia, Canada. He has since died, but the commune goes on. Another leader of the group is Ron Polack, who heads up the Ontological Society, the educational arm of the Emissaries. The Emissaries of Divine Light publish a magazine called *Integrity* and distribute it worldwide.

Recruiting into the Emissaries

Emissaries recruit mainly on university campuses, and

invite recruits to visit their communes and experience the life-style. Once convinced, recruits are told they must break away from society and their families to rid themselves of guilt. Blind obedience is stressed, and a very anti-intellectual approach is taken. No books, television, or radios are allowed.

Belief in Ontology

"Ontology" is a legitimate metaphysical term which usually means "the study of the ultimate nature of being." Ontology journals tell believers they have the potential to cure the sick with a natural current that is supposed to flow from their hands. The healing rituals practiced usually consist of waving their hands over a body, which action supposedly rids the body of evil spirits and disease. "Pneumaplasm" is a term used by this group and is supposedly the connecting force between the human body and spirit.

There is much written in Emissary publications of "radiation" which is supposedly the life-giving current flowing out of followers' hands. This radiation is supposed to work on the pneumaplasm and bring it into attunement or harmony with God. The person is then cured—even of such diseases as cancer, it is claimed.

In reading Emissary literature, we find much mention of "being where you are," "finding your way to Cosmic awareness," etc. Terms such as "vibrations," "patterns," "focalization," and "oneness" are used. These are not Bible terms (although the Emissaries sometimes quote the Bible, and because of this some people assume they are Christian). They are not, since they teach the Eastern belief of reincarnation and have the following view of Jesus Christ.

What the Emissaries of Divine Light Think of Jesus Christ

In speaking of salvation, page 11 of *Ontological Thought* (vol. 3, no. 10), makes this point:

> It is not, as in traditional Christianity, merely a process of magical transformation by a supernatural deity through belief in the alleged atoning work of Jesus Christ on the cross. The individual in such a scheme of things becomes little more than a bystander, and, since a Savior has done for him what he himself needs to do, there is no reason whatsoever for him to move out of his state of sin and weakness.

So the Emissaries of Divine Light prefer to set aside the salvation provided through Jesus Christ and move themselves out of their own state of sin and weakness. We can only be saddened by this rejection of Jesus Christ and His free gift of salvation.

The Way International

The founder of "The Way," Victor Paul Wierwille, was raised in a strict fundamentalist atmosphere, attending Moody Bible Institute, the University of Chicago Divinity School, and Princeton Seminary where he received a master's degree. Rather than remaining a fundamentalist, Wierwille decided to burn his theological library and set out on his own independent path to discover the meaning of Scripture.

Wierwille testifies that in 1942, "God spoke to me audibly, just like I'm talking to you now. He said He would teach me the Word as it had not been known since the first century, if I would teach it to others." After this, Wierwille went on to deny the Trinity and the deity of Jesus Christ and set up courses to teach people to "speak in tongues."

Organization of "The Way"

A recruiting program called WOW was originally in operation, although its numbers and influence have declined greatly in recent years. WOW stood for "the Word over the World," and recruits were brought into a commune in a tree-inspired system. The "trunk" was the international headquarters, the "roots"—the board of directors, the "limb"—the state organization, the "branches"— the city-wide or regional ministries, the "twig"—the local fellowship meeting on campus or in a home, and finally the "leaf"—each individual believer.

The recruits who became "leaves" soon found out that they had to function on about four hours of sleep a night, do exercises, go to work, fellowship and learn, and subsist on a high-starch, low-protein diet. Persons leaving reported these conditions and said they were fatigued physically and mentally and had a great fear of Satan. Many young, idealistic adults got drawn into this group believing it was real Christianity in action but found themselves in bondage. Many left as the groups disbanded but still need help with the lingering effects.

The Family of Love
(The Children of God)

The founder of the Children of God, David Berg, was a former Christian and Missionary Alliance minister who began reaching out to the hippies of the sixties. The group was fundamentalist in the beginning, but has since degenerated into the occult. Berg retired in 1970, but runs his organization with "letters" which are regarded by his followers as on a par with the Bible. These letters are also sold to provide income.

Doctrines of the Family of Love

In March of 1974 under the title "Flirty Little Fishy," a new recruiting tool was encouraged. Women in the organization were to become "hookers for Jesus," and religious prostitution became a way of life both in the commune and outside. Berg's views on sex became increasingly perverted, from encouraging group sex in the meetings to encouraging lesbianism among the women. Berg himself claimed to have sex with "spirits."

In *Revolutionary Sex*, David Berg says,

> From personal revelations and Bible Study, I am convinced that Jesus Himself could have enjoyed His Father's creation of sexual activity with some of the women He lived with, particularly Mary and Martha, and yet without sin. Why should it have been sin for Christ to have enjoyed sex that He Himself created?

Interestingly, the Mormons (the Church of Jesus Christ of Latter-day Saints) also teach that Jesus had sex relations with both the Marys and Martha, but within the framework of multiple marriages.

Berg's obsession with sex and his flagrant breaking of Bible commands shows that he is not a man of God. He also prophesied falsely that America would be destroyed in 1974. He has set the date for Christ's return for 1993. Time generally takes care of false prophets such as Berg.

Hare Krishna (ISKCON)—International Society for Krishna Consciousness

Devotees of this movement revere their god, Krishna. They believe he literally came to earth in human shape (though not truly human) and walked the earth 5000 years ago. He is pictured dancing with 100 women at one time and his allure was so powerful that each of them believed he was dancing with her alone and each one experienced orgiastic bliss.

Usually in Hinduism we find the doctrine of an impersonal god, yet in this brand of Hinduism a personal god, Krishna, is worshiped. As the Christian feels about Jesus, so the followers feel about Krishna. Further beliefs of this group are outlined in their official *Back to the Godhead* magazine, which followers use to recruit members off the streets, campuses, and in airports. We used to be able to spot Krishna devotees by their partly shaven heads and ponytails (left so they could be resurrected by being pulled out of their graves by this hank of hair), but now some do not cut their hair or dress strangely, so they are more difficult to detect.

Life in the Krishna Commune

The recruit is invited to a "love feast" at the commune and sees people chanting, singing, and dancing about, seemingly very happy and spiritual. Being spiritual means getting to services at 4:30 A.M., chanting and meditating with their beads for two hours, and then attending classes. Strict rules are enforced: no illicit sex, no intoxication, no meat-eating, no gambling.

The freedom to marry within the commune is not always granted, and if it is, the couple must live together as brother and sister except for physical relations once a month on a night designated for fertility, and then only after chanting for five or six hours.

Krishna devotees also take regularly to the streets with their repetitive chanting, bringing recruits back with them. Some now witness without appearing too different from the general population, but they are also recruiting.

Witnessing to the Krishna Group

Often, a Christian can engage a Krishna devotee in conversation when he is away from the commune. Seek to establish common ground. Do not openly attack his beliefs, but remember that devotees do believe that Jesus was to be listened to, and that there is value in the Bible. Gently share what Jesus means to you, and then go on to the claims of Jesus in the Bible. Krishna devotees often require good Christian friends they can count on, should they desire to leave the commune. Often they are subjected to "prisoner" tactics if they begin to doubt. They are then kept under constant watch and have no normal clothes or money when they leave. Be prepared to be a good Samaritan and show Christ's love in practical ways.

The Divine Light Mission of the Guru Maharaj Ji

The Guru Maharaj Ji says of himself, "God is great, but Guru is greater than God, because if you go to Guru, Guru will show you God." The guru takes such titles to himself as "Lord of the Universe," "the one and only perfect master for this age," and "The Christ."

The group lives communally, working at outside jobs or drawing welfare benefits, and turning their money over to their organization. They spend a great deal of time practicing their own peculiar brand of meditation in front of their guru's picture. They regard him as "Christ."

While chanting and meditating, devotees report hearing music, seeing light, and tasting nectar. They even report that nectar runs down their throats during meditation. An investigation into this happening revealed that most followers had postnasal drip due to their poor diet, and this was the mysterious "nectar"!

The Guru Maharaj Ji regularly uses Bible terms such as "the Word," "baptism in the Holy Spirit," "the light," "the kingdom of heaven," but he has given them Hindu meanings. For example, "the Word" of John 1:1 was interpreted by him to mean the vibrations felt while meditating, signifying the presence of God. Correctly, "the Word" is the person of Jesus Christ (John 1:14).

Witnessing to Those in the Divine Light Mission

Most members are soft-spoken and not aggressive. They believe Jesus was a teacher and the Bible has truth, so it is good to focus your discussion on the second coming of Jesus Christ, dealing with such Scriptures as Revelation 1:7, "Behold, He is coming with the clouds, and every eye will see Him, even those who pierced Him; and all the tribes of the earth will mourn over Him."

Ask them kindly if this could really be the Guru Maharaj Ji arriving in his airplane from India, as he teaches. Did he really fulfill the Scriptural requirements? Many are very curious about these facts. Remember to be patient, as their restricted diet greatly affects their health and ability to concentrate.

The Church Universal and Triumphant
(Summit Lighthouse)

This communal group is headed up by Elizabeth Clare Prophet, who maintains absolute control over her followers. This group steadily gained momentum over the years by inviting recruits to hear messages from an assortment of "ascended masters," including one called Jesus. No expense was spared in their advertising to lure interested people. When dealing with the subject of Jesus, Elizabeth Clare Prophet usually dwells on the supposed "lost years" of Jesus. She combines out-of-context Scripture references with mystical and occult views of Christ, usually revealed to her by her "ascended masters." Since the Bible forbids communication with the dead and the consulting of mediums (Deuteronomy 18:10-12), the Christian should avoid this group for that reason alone.

The Church Universal and Triumphant also practices "chanting" and "decreeing." "Chanting" is a noisy group activity which begins in English but builds to a higher and higher pitch, and ends up in an unintelligible jibberish. In addition to these emotion-charged meetings, each devotee is also taught to speak forth "decrees" and "fiats" designed to supposedly change the condition of the world by the spoken word. Perhaps the most disturbing chanting to the Christian is the repetition of the phrase "I AM THAT I AM." The devotee believes this confirms his own deity, but in the Bible this is the exclusive name of God (see Exodus 3:13-15). Such blasphemous chanting is offensive to true Christians.

In recent years Elizabeth Clare Prophet, believing Armageddon or the end of the world was going to occur on April 23, 1990, moved her followers to a large ranch in Montana. *MacLeans Magazine*, May 7, 1990, reported that some 2000 followers each paid $12,000 to this guru in order to have a space in the bomb shelters constructed on the property. The ranch was turned into an armed camp and the group got themselves in trouble with the law for their arsenal of weapons and ammunition.

When the foretold nuclear war did not occur as "guru Ma" Elizabeth Clare Prophet had foretold, she had a ready explanation to the charge of being a false prophet. She congratulated her group, saying their prayers had averted a nuclear first-strike by the Soviets!

There have been many TV shows and magazine articles exposing the control tactics of this group. We can only hope many followers will see the group for what it is and leave. Christians should be ready to expose the Scripture twisting of Elizabeth Clare Prophet, and gently share the real Jesus Christ with these hurting people. Remember that people with spiritual hunger are attracted to these groups, believing they are of God. They are still spiritually hungry when they leave.

The Late Bhagwan Shree Rajneesh and His Orange People

We are pleased to report that this destructive cult has greatly diminished in size. At one time it controlled the entire town of Antelope, Oregon, but its commune is now abandoned and its leader dead. His end came not long after the United States Air Force brought down two planes loaded with jewels and money he had received from his deserted followers. A court case followed, with some of the commune's leaders given jail sentences. Rajneesh was heavily fined and deported. His followers scattered, many with venereal diseases and mental illnesses left over from the uninhibited sex and harmful psychology practiced in the commune. We were able to minister to some of these disillusioned people, and some are now healing spiritually and physically with the help of their true Savior, Jesus Christ. We can only hope that Christians will reach out to the others who are still searching for truth and "wandering in the wilderness" after their experiences.

A Word on Deprogramming

Some believe that the only way out of a communal cult group is by kidnapping the poor, programmed members and subjecting them to endless hours of deprogramming. We believe this is committing further violence against already damaged persons. The important thing is to remove them from the cult environment and, as a last resort, it may be necessary to take them off the streets, although this may produce legal problems, depending on where you live. We prefer to fight spiritual battles with spiritual weapons and have the families enter into earnest intercessory prayer on behalf of people trapped in a communal cult. We have found that the Lord is able to bring them out in various ways, and they will contact their families somehow.

Now you have them back. What should you do? In the early days after release, the people will be "zombie-like." Remember that they have had very little rest and a poor diet. Let them sleep and eat for the first few days, but it may be necessary to keep them confined and take away objects by which they could harm themselves. Some may continue to have frightening demonic experiences. Once they appear normal and rested is the time for "deprogramming."

Pray for the leading of the Holy Spirit in all that you do,

and do all in an attitude of love and affection. They need lots of attention and physical hugging, etc.

If the person is tormented or acting strangely, remove all vestiges of the cult influence—namely beads, rings, books, etc. You may need to contact a knowledgeable pastor or mature Christian to perform a demon deliverance. Not all need this procedure, but some do, particularly those deeply into meditation, with its "spirit-guides."

Have literature available showing the errors of the group, and have Bible passages ready to use if requested. Be continually in prayer and wait for the leading of the Holy Spirit to proceed. If you know someone who was once part of the group and left, you could ask for his help. It is much preferable if this person is now a Christian.

Some Christians have found it helpful to obtain literature dealing with mind control so they can understand what has happened to the personality of their loved ones.

Be encouraged that we have personally seen many "hopeless cases" respond to unconditional love and the gospel, and who are now radiant Christians out of these very groups. "With God all things are possible" (Matthew 19:26).

Chapter 7

THE EASTERN MEDITATION CULTS

For many years Christian churches have been sending missionaries over to heathen lands to bring the message of Jesus Christ. The tide has turned now, with the heathen lands sending their missionaries into "Christian" countries, bringing with them their personal brand of Hinduism. Many meditation groups have sprung up and infiltrated our government programs, schools, improvement courses, and even our churches.

At the roots of all these Eastern religions is basic Hinduism, or pantheism—that is, the belief that God is the sum of all beings, forces, etc., everything present in the universe. In Hinduism there is no evil, for how can God be evil? Since God is in everything and indeed is everything, He becomes an "it," an impersonal force.

The believer in Hinduism or one of its forms is always striving to be in tune with the cosmic force, which is god. This striving for "god-consciousness" is done by practicing a form of meditation.

Since this Eastern teaching of an impersonal god-force is not too palatable to the "Christian" countries who are used to a personal Savior who cares for them, a personal

God who loves them, some adaptations were needed to make Eastern religion palatable and acceptable to people in the "Christian" countries, many of them nominal Christians. This was accomplished in three ways.

1. Absorb the existing religion into Hinduism, which is full of endless philosophies anyway, and never ask the interested person to give up the God of their forefathers or the Jesus of their Sunday school youth. The meditation, it is promised, will draw you closer to your own God, your own religion. "You'll understand Jesus better" is the assurance.

2. Present a Christ-substitute to satisfy the Christian mind. Thus we see Sun Myung Moon of the Unification Church being presented as "Lord of the Second Advent." The Guru Maharaj Ji of the Divine Light Mission calls himself "Lord of the Universe" and "Perfect Master." Both are believed by their respective followers to be Christ come again. Meher Baba of Sufism Reoriented, Inc. stated, "There is no doubt of my being God personified, I am the Christ." The list goes on.

3. Incorporate Hinduism into seemingly nonreligious courses, such as est (Erhard Seminars Training), now presenting similar beliefs under the title "The Forum." Similar groups are Lifespring, Assertiveness Training, Personal Growth Seminars, etc.

Unsuspecting people now swarm to absorb Hinduism in its various disguises, signing up and paying for "assertiveness" courses, taking Yoga, and tuning out stress with meditation. Most YMCAs, supposedly Christian organizations, routinely offer Yoga classes. To understand all of this, we need to look at the "granddaddy" of all Hindu deception: Transcendental Meditation.

Transcendental Meditation (TM)

Transcendental Meditation began with Maharishi Mahesh Yogi, who originated the movement in 1958 and moved to the United States in 1961. He claims to follow his departed leader (master, god) the Guru Dev. Guru Dev's picture adorns TM altars.

Deceptive Recruiting Techniques

Transcendental Meditation and its successors are always presented as a "technique" and never as a religion. Christians and non-Christians alike are encouraged to practice a form of meditation as a relief from stress, to lower blood pressure, improve mental health, and even improve their sex life. "It's not a religion" they are repeatedly told; it's a technique that won't interfere with your own beliefs or lack of beliefs, your life-style, or your job. It's so beneficial, just a few minutes a day repeating a "mantra" will enable you to "transcend" all your troubles, and you will have peace, joy, good health, etc. Sounds good, so why not?

The Ritual of Initiation into TM

The person is convinced and finds himself at the ritual of initiation, which he must go through before he receives his promised "mantra." He is taught how to participate, but can't understand a word that's being said as it's all in a foreign language. The English translation is never given, even if the initiate asks. The initiate notices an altar with a picture of a guru on it. The ceremony begins. There are three phases to the ceremony.

1. *Recitation of Names.* These are the names of "the apostolic succession through which the holy knowledge of the TM mantras has been passed." All names are considered to be gods and worthy of worship. There are over 20 Hindu gods to acknowledge in this ceremony, and here are some of the attributes given to them. Reverently and worshipfully, they are called variously "Redeemer," "Emancipator of the world," "Supreme Teacher full of brilliance," "the Pure," "Adorned with immeasurable glory," etc. These are sufficient to show that titles that should be used for the one God of the Bible are used instead for Hindu gods. The initiate, however, is blissfully unaware of this, since he doesn't understand the language.

2. *Offerings in the TM Ceremony.* There are 17 different items offered in turn. Here the initiate puts three of these objects (a handkerchief, flowers, and fruit) on the altar at the proper time—an offering to the Hindu gods just named, as personified by the guru pictured. One would expect that some Sunday school lesson might come into the initiate's mind about idolatry and offerings to idols, but few make the connection at this point.

3. *Hymn of Praise and Adoration.* This hymn is offered to Guru Dev in his status as deity, as recognized by classical Hinduism (Brahma, Vishnu and Shiva, with Shiva being evil). The initiate is then invited to follow in his teacher's example and bow down before the Guru Dev. This is a bit much for some initiates who were told it wasn't a religion, so if they hesitate, they are not forced to bow.

The offerings must be made, however. Now the initiate prepares to receive his secret "mantra."

What Is the "Mantra"?

The mantra is a word or series of words that the initiate must repeat over and over again until he really "enters in" and "transcends" into a trancelike state. His teacher stays with him until he is sure this state is reached. Eventually the sound of the mantra and his thoughts cease, and the initiate "transcends" into a new dimension, ready for new "spiritual experiences."

What an initiate does not know is this mantra that he is repeating over and over again is really the name of one of the millions of gods of Hinduism. As the initiate takes up this practice, he will in time be visited by a "spirit-guide," often bearing the name he has been calling. As he is now proficient at making his mind blank and empty, the spirit-guide urges him to yield to his influence. What began in bliss may end in a nightmare of demon possession, mind control, and torment.

Link Between Drugs and Meditation

It is an interesting fact that those practicing Eastern meditation often meet the same spirit-guides as those who do no meditation, but take mind-altering drugs. This is no surprise to Bible students, for they recognize these spirit-guides for what they are—manifestations of demons.

The whole Transcendental Meditation ceremony can be summed up in one biblical term: idolatry (Leviticus 26:1). Do not be deceived: Transcendental Meditation is a religion and not just a technique.

Examining Eckankar—
the Ancient Art
of Soul-Travel

Eckankar, also called "The Path to Total Awareness," was introduced to the United States by a man named Paul Twitchell. He had trained under a Tibetan mystic, Rebazar Tarz, and reportedly received the "spiritual mantle of Mahanta," thus making him the living Eckankar master. When Twitchell died in 1971, the mantle supposedly fell on Darwin Gross. Harold Klemp is the present leader.

The Promises of Eckankar

Eckankar's message is spread by flashy advertising displays in public places, by billboards, and by newspaper ads. Typical of their advertising pitch is the statement on the back of their popular book *The Tiger's Fang* by Paul Twitchell:

> You are about to enter a strange new world with one of the most astonishing prophets of the century.... Discover the fabulous Mountain of Light...explore the Universal Mind...find out how you too, can travel outside of space, time and causation...and much more.

These promises lure the reader on to explore the claims of Eckankar, which claims to be the fountainhead of all religions and philosophies. "All is One," they proclaim, and each can find "a" way to God. The best way, they claim, is to look into the mystical teachings of the East and pay close attention to the Eckankar masters.

Empty Your Mind—Stop Thinking!

In *The Tiger's Fang*, page 42, we are told,

> By putting a stop to all analytic thinking, in the certain knowledge that there is nothing which has an absolute existence, nothing on which to lay hold, nothing on which to rely, nothing in which to abide, nothing subjective or objective, then they cross the dark region of this world and come to my temple in the pine grove. Then I will give them the true light and send them upward to the region of the great Lord Sohang.

In other words, once you have turned your mind off and left it blank and empty, you are promised a fabulous experience—soul-travel—which will result in true light at the end.

The Experience of Soul-Travel

Eckankar philosophy teaches that the physical world is an illusion which one needs to escape through a process called "soul-travel." This technique is supposed to be taught only by Eckankar teachers or masters, but in fact is found in other Eastern groups also. Participants really believe they have an out-of-body "soul-travel" experience when they yield to their spirit-guides or spirit-travelers, who take them on these "trips." These "travel guides" are contacted in altered states of consciousness.

From our conversations with Eckankar devotees, including those who have discontinued association with the group, a pattern of common experiences emerges.

The initial experiences are usually blissful and the spirit-guides wonderful. However, as the person yields, the spirit-guides take ever-increasing control over the life and soul-travels of the person. Often the person ends up being controlled totally by the spirit-guide(s), and can even be forced to take "bad trips." Often this cycle is broken only when deliverance is performed in the name of Jesus Christ by Christians. Christians recognize these spirit-guides to be demons.

Christians well know that they are not to have empty minds, as Eckankar advocates. We are told in 2 Timothy 2:15 to "be diligent" or "study." We are to renew our minds (Romans 12:2), and we are to even have "the mind of Christ" (1 Corinthians 2:16). By filling our minds with Bible truths, we are forewarned that Satan can come disguised as an "angel of light" (2 Corinthians 11:14,15). We also find out that what may appear to be light can, in fact, be darkness (Luke 11:34,35).

The Forum and est: ## Erhard Seminars Training

The founder of est is Werner Erhard (formerly Jack Rosenberg). Erhard came out of a background of Scientology and Mind Dynamics, mixed with extensive occult involvement. He studied Zen Buddhism, hypnosis, Subud, Yoga, Silva Mind Control, psychocybernetics, Gestalt, encounter therapy, and transpersonal psychology. His own brand of this mixture turned out to be est, now updated and re-presented as "The Forum" by some of his followers.

The official biographer of Werner Erhard, a Mr. Bartley, made this statement, "The responsible person does not hunger and thirst after righteousness." Compare this with the statement of our Lord Jesus Christ as recorded in

Matthew 5:6, "Blessed are those who hunger and thirst for righteousness, for they shall be satisfied."

Although The Forum claims to be nonreligious, it is in fact thinly veiled Hinduism mixed with mind control—or basically est under another name.

What Happened in est?

The est seminars were an intensive 60-hour time of psychological indoctrination designed to restructure a person's worldview. Est seminars have been held in prisons and police forces, and clergy received a 50 percent discount! What happened at these intense seminars?

The 60-hour experience transformed people because through intensive and at times brutal and cruel physical and mental conditioning, the individual underwent a "conversion episode," where the old way of viewing reality was supplanted with the est way. As one est trainer so aptly put it, "We're gonna throw away your whole belief system—we're gonna tear you down and put you back together" (*Psychology Today*, 8/75, p. 39).

In the est seminar, participants were subjected to tensions, harassment, deliberately foul language, and trauma. The bombarding with foul language was kept up until the person became numb and, after a period of time, ceased to be shocked by it and, in fact, became passively, wearily open to it. Compare this to Ephesians 4:29, "Let no unwholesome word proceed from your mouth, but only such a word as is good for edification according to the need of the moment, that it may give grace to those who hear."

The est View of God

One unsuspecting Christian, who found himself locked in at a seminar and shocked by the goings-on, raised his hand and asked, "What about God?" The instructor replied, "I don't know if there is a God, but if there is, she's black!" The Christian faith takes a lot of mocking at these seminars, and its values are ridiculed.

Erhard published a list called "Rules About Life." Rule number one states that life has no rules, and all the other numbers are blank. Persons attending are told that they must become gods themselves. Est denies that there is evil and claims the universe is perfect. Christians will recognize the original lie of Satan the devil in the garden, where he promised Eve she could become "as god" or "like God" (Genesis 3:5). Erhard goes on to admit in his writings that he finds it difficult to deal with people who have a belief in God.

Although a Christian believer is told est will not interfere with his religious beliefs, this is simply not true. Est may claim to be nonreligious, but upon examination its concept is totally religious, attempting to replace belief in a personal God who loves and cares for us with the impersonal, pantheistic god of Hinduism.

Est teaches that one cannot look to any supreme being for special treatment, goodness, or award. Looking to the Bible, we find this opposite statement in Hebrews 11:6: "And without faith it is impossible to please Him, for he who comes to God must believe that He is, and that He is a rewarder of those who seek Him."

Est teaches that each person controls his own universe and destiny. This teaching automatically turns hearers away from Christ. Est believers would see no need whatsoever to turn to a Savior since they believe they are God, there is no sin, and anything goes. Beware of the Forum, run mostly by est graduates.

The est or Forum seminars are no place for a Christian. Other people are drawn there because there is a spiritual hunger in their lives. Some seek to be more assertive or to control their lives by being more aggressive.

Est is not the answer to lasting satisfaction, but Jesus Christ is. Every person is looking for peace in his life and wants to live life abundantly, not just exist. Christ invites us to be true sons of God by receiving Him into our lives and hearts (John 1:12,13). Only then will we know real peace within—the kind God provides (John 14:27).

Yoga Exercises and the Christian

Yoga exercises sound so beneficial. Bookshops and libraries are full of Yoga books. Doctors, clergy, teachers, and professional people practice it. Yoga claims to work on the muscular, glandular, and physical nervous systems. Wonderful physical and emotional benefits are promised. Indeed, Yoga is a complex subject, with many different types, but we will deal at this time solely with the Christian view of Yoga. Many Christians practicing Yoga have expressed indignation when its connections to Hinduism and Eastern mystical religions are pointed out. Some Christians even declare that when they are relaxing or practicing Yoga postures, they keep their thoughts on Jesus and are therefore protected. Both Christians and Yoga teachers are heard to loudly deny that Yoga is any kind of religion, but rather a beneficial exercise.

Principles Behind Yoga Exercises

In truth, Yoga exercises are *not* just of a physical nature. They cannot be separated from their mystical, Hinduistic purposes. Yoga teaches that there are some 72,000 invisible psychic channels, which constitute an other-dimensional body. This "subtle" body is claimed to connect to the real body in seven predominate places, ranging from the base of the spine to the top of the head. The teachings of Hatha (physical) Yoga teach that at the base of the spine lies coiled a great serpent power called kundalini.

A former Yoga teacher for ten years and former vice-principal of a large Yoga school, who is now a Christian, comments:

> Every posture is designed to stimulate this power to uncoil itself and rise up through the nerve centres in the spine, which are closely related to the endocrine glands, until it finally reaches the pituitary gland—the thousand petal lotus—and when this occurs after long and disciplined practice, perfect enlightenment is achieved.

A Christian need not be instructed on the significance of the original serpent, Satan the devil (see Revelation 12:9)!

The Purpose of Yoga

The purpose of Yoga exercises is to align the "subtle" body with the real one and thereby alter the consciousness of the practitioner in a specified way. The positioning of the body in the Yoga postures opens up the practitioner to "vibrations" which teach him the "wisdom" of Yoga. As a person proceeds with the physical Yoga exercises, it will not be too long before he is asked to practice "meditation" along with the postures. Often this begins with just an urging to "empty the mind of all thought," and then progresses into real Hindu meditation. Christian meditation as taught throughout the Bible is a *filling* of the mind with the words and precepts of God, and is the exact opposite of Yoga meditation.

Physical But Not Spiritual?

Skeptical Christians should go to their public library and read any authoritative book on Hatha Yoga (physical Yoga). These various books make it clear that physical Yoga is just the first step to spiritual Yoga, and its roots are solidly in Hinduism. One Christian authority on Yoga, Mother Basilea Schlink of the Darmstat Sisters, warns in a pamphlet, "Every Yoga posture was originally designed to worship the Hindu god Krishna."

Yoga's Views of Jesus Christ

Jesus Christ is presented by Yoga as just one of the many great masters like Buddha, Krishna, and Mohammed. Yoga teaches that there are many ways of reaching God, all equally good. If Christians are seeking peace and relaxation in Yoga, then they are seeking the world's way, not the way of Jesus Christ. John 14:27 puts it well, quoting Jesus Christ, "Peace I leave with you; My peace I give to you; not as the world gives, do I give to you. Let not your heart be troubled, nor let it be fearful."

The true peace from Jesus Christ sustains the Christian through all circumstances, not just while exercising or meditating. Christians practicing Yoga need to cease immediately, repent of it, and ask God's forgiveness. Yoga is not just exercise!

Examining Scientology

The late L. Ron Hubbard, the founder of Scientology, declared, "Writing for a penny a word is ridiculous. If a man really wants to make a million, the best way would be to start his own religion." Hubbard did just that, and his organization has reportedly grossed as much as $100 million in a year.

Examining L. Ron Hubbard

Hubbard's personal background is a sham. Despite his claim that he was 74 trillion years old, counting his past lives, the public record shows differently! When he claimed to be learning the secrets of life from lamas, magicians, and priests in Asia and the South Pacific during 1925 to 1929, he was actually a mediocre high school student. His claims to doctorates in divinity and philosophy are fictitious. According to the *Los Angeles Times*, his college transcript shows he dropped out of his sophomore year at George Washington University. His claim to be a World War II hero, miraculously curing himself of near-fatal combat wounds, is just as bogus. Hubbard never saw combat and was discharged from the Navy in 1946. It was now time to start his own religion.

Doctrines of Scientology

In 1950 Hubbard published his book *Dianetics: The Modern Science of Mental Health*. This same book is now being extensively distributed as a "bestseller." Hubbard also published a book called *Scientology: A History of Man*. Hubbard established his church in 1952 and used it as a vehicle for applying principles contained in his books. Scientology best fits in the category of science fiction, with strong mystical overtones, even though it is presented as a cure for mental problems. Hubbard built such a strong organization that it has survived his death and continues to flourish. Many people are drawn in due to several prominent celebrities who belong. Each level in Scientology costs the participant progressively more money to find out the following doctrines.

The Thetan Gods Doctrine

Scientology teaches that each of us is, in fact, a fallen god. "Thetans" were supposedly heroes of a long-lost intergalactic civilization slaughtered by evil forces 40 million year ago. The "Thetan" spirit supposedly resides within each one of us, but is well hidden by traumas in repeated cycles of reincarnation. It is Scientology's purpose to offer release of a person's past traumas so that he may realize that he is indeed a god, a "Thetan."

The Road to Perfection via Scientology

Scientology teaches that the "Thetan within" can be freed by help from one of their counselors using an electro-galvanometer (E-Meter), which is basically a needle wired to two tin cans. The subject is regressed into his "past lives" over a period of expensive sessions, until he is freed from his past traumas (engrams). The subject is then declared to be a "Thetan," in control of the physical realm of the universe, and can experience "soul-travel."

Bible Warnings Against Scientology Practices

The first and most obvious warning would be the words of Jesus Christ, "Many false prophets shall rise, and shall deceive many" (Matthew 24:11 KJV). Hubbard was not truthful to his followers from the very beginning regarding his background. The teaching that we have past lives called reincarnations is also false. Hebrews 9:27 declares, "It is appointed unto men once to die, but after this the judgment" (KJV).

The teaching that we can become "gods" or "Thetans" is a repeat of the original lie by Satan the devil to Eve in the Garden of Eden (Genesis 3:5). Almighty God has an exclusive claim on "Godship." He is the only true God. All other gods—even those mentioned in the Bible—are false.

Practicing Scientology will not bring you closer to the true God of the Bible. You need the true Jesus Christ of the Bible to be your mediator: "For there is one God, and one mediator between God and men, the man Christ Jesus" (1 Timothy 2:5 KJV).

Christians should be aware that Scientology is also operating or influencing the following organizations: Advanced Organization of Los Angeles (AOLA); Author Services Inc.; Dianetics; Flag Service Organization; Freewinds Relay Office; Narconaon; Sterling Management; and Wise Understanding.

A Christian View of Meditation

Since there are so many "meditation" cults in evidence today, should Christians avoid anything to do with meditation? No, for the Bible encourages meditation done God's way. What is the difference?

Godly meditation is a filling of the mind with the word of God (Psalm 119:15,16). It is never the mindless repeating of a word or words until a trancelike state is produced, as in Eastern meditation. Eastern meditation is an emptying of the mind to allow the infiltration of influences from spirit-guides (demons). It bears no resemblance to Christian, biblical meditation.

Christian Meditation the Bible Way

1. Our meditation must be acceptable to God (Psalm 19:14).

2. Meditation is a time to review what our minds have been taught (Joshua 1:8).

3. It is proper to meditate concerning God Himself (Psalm 63:5,6).

4. We are to take "every thought captive to the obedience of Christ" (2 Corinthians 10:5). This increases the effectiveness of our spiritual warfare.

5. We are to be absorbed in reading of the Scripture, exhortation, and teaching, as well as the "spiritual gift within [us]" (1 Timothy 4:13-16). This type of "absorption" will result in salvation to those who hear us.

A great prophet of God wrote in Isaiah 40:31, "Yet those who wait for the Lord will gain new strength; they will mount up with wings like eagles, they will run and not get tired, they will walk and not become weary."

Christian meditation is a real time of communication with God, and is even akin to prayer. "Let my meditation be pleasing to Him; as for me, I shall be glad in the Lord" (Psalm 104:34).

Truly, Christians need to be aware of subtle Eastern religious influences in our workplaces, schools, and even our churches. Our children need to be educated so they can avoid involvement in these practices.

Chapter 8

EXAMINING THE NEW AGE MOVEMENT

The term "New Age" has saturated the media for some time now. One can hardly turn on a talk show without being bombarded with some aspect of the "New Age," be it "channeling" or "holistic health" or "astral travel." The so-called "New Age" is big business. *Time* magazine (Dec. 7, 1987) reported that Bantam Books had a tenfold increase in New Age titles in the past decade and that New Age bookstores have doubled in the past five years to total about 2500. The "Grammy Awards" have a special prize now for "New Age music."

Shirley MacLaine, a prominent New Ager, is quoted in this same *Time* magazine as saying, "I want to prove that spirituality is profitable." Also, "If you don't see me as God," says MacLaine, blithe as ever, "it's because you don't see yourself as God" (*Time* magazine, Dec. 7, 1987, p. 68).

One thing is certain: People are flocking to the New Age Movement, or to various parts of it, looking for answers in this life, and the Christian must be prepared to deal with New Age concepts and understand them if we are to offer these honest, seeking persons a better alternative.

Defining the New Age Movement

It is difficult to place a firm definition on the New Age Movement because it encompasses so many concepts. It mixes revived Gnosticism and Eastern mysticism with health and well-being treatments, and includes astrology and even mediumship, or channeling. Not all persons believe all aspects of the New Age, but many people practice some of them. We will therefore briefly list some of the identifying marks of the New Age Movement and present a Christian, biblical perspective.

Surface "Respect for All Religions"

Christians will notice right away how difficult it is to witness to a person who has had various experiences in the New Age. When presented with Christian counsel, the New Ager often will reply, "I'll allow you your truth, and you allow me mine." This "reasoning" flies in the face of the meaning of the word "truth." The *Doubleday Dictionary* defines "truth" as "conformity to fact or reality."

The Christian will wish to use the Bible as "fact" to establish "truth," while the New Ager will wish to use his "experience(s)" to establish "truth." He may even deny reality altogether. New Agers do not want to hear that anything is necessarily "right" or "wrong," "good" or "evil," as each wants to be God and make his own decisions. In our experience, we have usually had to wait until the New Ager has had a bad "trip" with his seeking and has succeeded in finding out that he no longer has control. Then he wants help, and he wants out! Persons out of a Christian background who ignorantly become involved in New Age activities are often convicted of violating Bible principles when these are lovingly pointed out to them with a real concern for their spiritual well-being.

New Age View of God

The New Age Movement has the Eastern view of God, namely that "God is all" and "man is God." Since they believe that God is the sum total of all things, then there is no evil nor any standards to live by, according to their reasoning. They are constantly trying to draw closer to the "god-force" or "energy" by their various techniques. Indeed, they hope to enter the godhead.

The Bible view is the exact opposite. We worship a personal God, who is the Creator of all. Romans 1:20-23 says,

> For since the creation of the world His invisible attributes, His eternal power and divine nature, have been clearly seen, being understood through what has been made, so that they are without excuse. For even though they knew God, they did not honor Him as God, or give thanks; but they became futile in their speculations, and their foolish heart was darkened. Professing to be wise, they became fools, and exchanged the glory of the incorruptible God for an image in the form of corruptible man.

There is only one Scripture in the Bible where humans were told they could become gods, and that was when Satan the devil lied to the gullible and foolish Eve (Genesis 3:4,5).

New Age View of the Person of Jesus Christ

New Age teaching presents Jesus Christ as a "world teacher," an "ascended master," a man with "Christ principle," a "cosmic Christ." The Bible presents Jesus Christ as Almighty God manifest in the flesh (see John 1:1,14). Quite a difference!

I like to ask New Agers, "Would Jesus Christ teach truth or error?" They admit that He would teach truth. Then the Christian is in a position to present the claims of Jesus Christ as to who He is. You may find the points brought out in chapter 9, "Defending the Deity of Jesus Christ to the Cults," very helpful in these cases.

Looking for Messiah

Most New Agers are expecting "Messiah" to reveal himself any day now. Most believe he is already alive and living somewhere in the world. Those believing the date 1982 for his revealing already have "egg on their faces" for spending thousands of dollars to take out a full-page ad in major newspapers in major cities worldwide to announce the arrival of the "Maitreya" or "Messiah." Followers were blamed for the failure by creating enough positive "energy," so the date has been moved forward, rather indefinitely at this point.

This view does not surprise Bible students as they have been forewarned in 1 John 4:1-3:

> Beloved, do not believe every spirit, but test
> the spirits to see whether they are from God;
> because many false prophets have gone out into
> the world. By this you know the Spirit of God:

every spirit that confesses that Jesus Christ has come in the flesh is from God; and every spirit that does not confess Jesus is not from God; and this is the spirit of the antichrist, of which you have heard that it is coming, and now it is already in the world.

We sincerely believe that New Agers have been deceived into anticipating the arrival of the Antichrist.

New Age "Salvation by Self"

The New Age Movement is extremely humanistic. Since each person believes he is a god and in charge of his own universe, it follows that he can "work out his own salvation" and has no need of a Savior. He is therefore continually "tuning in" with meditation and striving to become part of the god-force. While missing the true Jesus Christ of the Bible, he tunes in various "spirit-guides" and accepts the experiences they give him as "truth." He imagines he is making progress toward salvation, or self-realization. The Bible, once again, presents the opposite view. Rather than being self-sufficient gods, the Bible teaches that we are humans who have all inherited sin from our common forefather, Adam. Romans 5:12 reads, "Therefore, just as through one man sin entered the world, and death through sin, and so death spread to all men, because all sinned."

We truly cannot save ourselves. We may seek in various experiences for light, but Jesus Christ is the true light. John 1:9, referring to Jesus Christ, reads, "There was the true light which, coming into the world, enlightens every man." Verses 12 and 13 of John 1 also promise,

> But as many as received Him [Jesus Christ], to
> them He gave the right to become children of
> God, even to those who believe in His name, who
> were born not of blood, nor of the will of the flesh,
> nor of the will of man, but of God.

Those seeking for a better life can find it in the person of
Jesus Christ who promises in John 10:10, "I came that
they might have life, and might have it abundantly."

Channeling—An Enlightening Experience or a Dangerous Practice?

Channeling is a popular new word for an ancient experience—that of allowing oneself to be a spirit medium and
have voices supposedly from the dead speak through you.
The person lapses into a trance and has no remembrance
of the experience afterward. No matter how famous or
obscure the medium is, the messages delivered are all
similar—namely, that you are God, there is no sin or punishment, good or evil, and Jesus is not the only Son of God.
Egos are often inflated by claims that the person was
somebody famous in a past life. Great wisdom from ages
past is supposedly imparted, but in fact is usually vague
and disjointed.

The Bible strongly warns against contacting spirits
through mediums. Leviticus 19:31 says, "Do not turn to
mediums or spiritists; do not seek them out to be defiled by
them. I am the Lord your God."

God lovingly protects us from demon spirits (the New
Age word is "entities"), and anyone foolish enough to dab-
ble in the occult in this manner is asking for, at the very
least, demon oppression, and very possibly, demon possession. Deliverance is possible, however, in the name of the
true Jesus Christ.

Tuning Out with Eastern Meditation and Mantras

We have dealt with this subject in chapter 7, "The Eastern Meditation Cults," so will comment briefly here. Emptying the mind in an altered state of consciousness and calling on gods or entities will result in the entities visiting you to guide you spiritually into new, and often frightening experiences.

Bible meditation is the filling of your mind with the truth of God's Word and reflecting on what you have learned. True meditation, done God's way, will protect you from the dangerous, counterfeit meditation of the New Age Movement.

Holistic Health Warnings

On the surface, holistic health sounds wonderful. It makes sense to treat the whole person—spirit, soul, and body—to ensure good health. However, many questionable practices have crept into the attempt to treat the whole person. Often one finds a medically untrained psychic doing the diagnosis, perhaps with the aid of a "spirit-guide" or an "entity" posing as a doctor from a former life.

Often Eastern meditation is prescribed, or a diet lacking in essential nutrition. Medically unproven practices abound, such as iridology (examining the iris to diagnose ailments all over the body) or kinesiology (the testing of muscles and body balances), and homeopathy (the treating of ailments with small amounts of poisons to build up a resistance), or reflexology (the treating of all bodily ailments by massaging various areas of the feet). Of themselves, these treatments may be of some help, but one should examine carefully the beliefs and spiritual practices of the person performing these treatments.

For example, some years ago I went to a chiropractor for a neck problem. He professed to be a Christian but had Eastern-type posters on his wall saying things like "The Force be with you."

When questioned closely by me, he admitted that he was trying to align my spine so my "energy flow" would be attuned to the universal energy and not be impeded. I promptly left and sought treatment from a chiropractor without these New Age spiritual overtones.

Christians need to inquire carefully beyond surface appearances and choose treatment that will not violate their Christian values or open them up to oppression by the forces of darkness.

Belief in Reincarnation

Many today are turning their attention to practitioners who promise to "regress them to their past lives" and deal with lingering traumas from past lives so they will feel better today. This practice is based on the Hindu doctrine of reincarnation, that when you die your soul is reborn in another human. In other words, you recycle after death— no heaven or hell, just go around again!

New Agers claim without one shred of evidence that the teaching of reincarnation was removed from the Bible at the Council of Nicea in A.D. 325. What nonsense! The Council of Nicea dealt with the Arian heresy and the deity of Jesus Christ. Also, if this claim is correct, then how come recent finds of extremely ancient copies of the biblical Scriptures contain no references to reincarnation? I would suggest that New Agers spend some time in their local libraries finding out the truth about this important matter. The Bible, in fact, teaches the opposite of reincarnation.

Hebrews 9:27 (KJV) plainly states: "It is appointed unto men *once* to die, but after this the judgment" (emphasis added).

Is Reincarnation "Proved" by Altered States of Consciousness?

Hypnotism plays a large part in so-called regressions to a former life. Admittedly, some believe they really have been regressed and have even given correct details of someone's past life while in an altered state of consciousness. Could this be because the demons have knowledge at their disposal to deceive man? The Bible warns in 1 Timothy 4:1, "But the [Holy] Spirit explicitly says that in later times some will fall away from the faith, paying attention to deceitful spirits and doctrines of demons."

Is Reincarnation Logical?

If souls merely recycle (to new humans only, according to reincarnation), why then is the world's population increasing if the same number of souls are going round and round? Also, the birthrate exceeds the death rate, so where are these supposedly newly reincarnated souls coming from? Also, shouldn't we see some evidence of our natures improving after so much purifying?

Beware of the misuse of Bible texts to try to prop up these nonbiblical teachings. In context, there is not one Scripture to support this belief. It is clearly not of God and should be avoided.

The List Goes On and On

New Agers also involve themselves in astrology, reading crystals, color therapy, dream studies, tarot cards, psychic readings, faith healings, psychic surgery, extrasensory perception (ESP), and even UFOs. Not all New Agers participate in all these things, but it is certainly a mixed bag and a mixed group.

Some Groups Encompassing Some Aspects of New Age Theology

This is not a complete list by any means, but we hope it helps you identify some of these groups and practices: Theosophical Society, Christian Science, Unity School of Christianity, Findhorn, Chinook Learning Center, ESP, Transcendental Meditation, Eckankar, The Forum (est), Silva Mind Control, Lifespring, Pacific Institute, numerology, Scientology, Yoga, Academy of Universal Truth, Kabalah, Masons, astrology, Baha'i Faith, Aetherius Society, Anthroposophical Society, Edgar Cayce (Association for Research and Enlightenment), Astara, Baba Ram Dass (Hanuman Foundation), Bawa Muhaiyaddeen Fellowship, The Holy Order of Mans, "I AM" Movement, Inner Peace Movement, International Community of Jesus (The Jamilians), Jainism, Megiddo Mission, Psychiana, Radha Soami Society, Rajneesh, Rosicrucians, Ruhani Satsang, Sathya Sai Baba, Self-Realization Fellowship, Spiritual Advancement of the Individual Foundation, Spiritual Frontiers Fellowship, spiritualists, occult, Sri Chinmoy Centers, Still Point Institute, Subud, Sufism, Summit Lighthouse, Swami Kriyananda Taoism, Unitarian–Universalist Association, Zoroastrianism. There are many others.

In Conclusion

The New Age Movement is not new at all, but is Eastern mysticism and the occult, blended in with humanism. The Christian should not have part in any aspect of it. It has even crept into the Christian church, with some TV teachers promising you can be "a god," and some "inner healing" seminars dabbling in areas they should be avoiding. Christian bookstores should take responsibility and rid their shelves of Eastern-influence books masquerading as Christianity. "Do not be bound together with unbelievers; for what partnership have righteousness and lawlessness, or what fellowship has light with darkness?" (2 Corinthians 6:14).

Chapter 9

DEFENDING THE DEITY OF JESUS CHRIST TO THE CULTS

But sanctify Christ as Lord in your hearts, always being ready to make a defense to everyone who asks you to give an account for the hope that is in you, yet with gentleness and reverence (1 Peter 3:15).

I f we hope to effectively win souls for Christ out of the cults, we must be ready to defend the deity of Christ above all else, for Christ is always misrepresented by the cult groups. This misrepresentation usually takes the form of denying His deity. In the world of the cults, they either deify man or humanize God. We need to present them with the right Jesus Christ since they have "another Jesus" (2 Corinthians 11:4).

Presenting the True Jesus Christ

The Jesus Christ of the Bible is truly God and yet truly man, and both these aspects need to be dealt with to clear up the confusion in the cultists' minds.

In our human thinking, which is finite, we cannot always understand the infinite God. However, He has revealed Himself through the pages of the Bible, and we must either accept the revelation of Himself that He has made or resort to manmade doctrines and concepts. Most cults will accept the Bible as an authority, so we may proceed.

Believing John 1:1 As Written

"In the beginning was the Word, and the Word was with God, and the Word was God." In our human thinking, we say, "Wait a minute, how can the Word be *with* God and yet *be* God, since there is only *one God*?" Our human understanding is just not up to this statement. We know *we* can't be "with" someone, and yet "be" that someone, but remember, God does not have our limitations! God reveals Himself this way throughout Scripture. An example is Isaiah 44:6: "Thus says the Lord [YHWH], the King of Israel and his Redeemer, the Lord [YHWH] of hosts [sounds like two, but . . .]: 'I am the first and I am the last, and there is no God besides Me.'"

We must either accept this truth or reject it. Let's choose to accept the fact that God says there is only one God and that the "Word was God." This is what the early church did, although they did not fully understand it. We find what I like to call an early creed of the church—a common confession—in 1 Timothy 3:16,

> And by common confession great is the mystery of godliness: He who was revealed in the flesh, was vindicated in the Spirit, beheld by angels, proclaimed among the nations, believed on in the world, taken up in glory (1 Timothy 3:16).

Knowing God's Mystery: Jesus Christ

Just because Jesus Christ is called a "mystery," it doesn't mean that we can never know Him or understand how He can be truly God and truly man at the same time. Colossians 2:2 promises,

> That their hearts may be encouraged, having been knit together in love, and attaining to all the wealth that comes from the full assurance of understanding, resulting in a *true knowledge* of God's mystery, that is, Christ Himself (emphasis added).

Jesus Christ Is Almighty God

We need to make the vital point at the very beginning that Jesus Christ is Almighty God. He is not some secondary god or one of many gods, but really is the one true Almighty God. Christians believe Jesus Christ is Almighty God manifest in the flesh. What follows is a good presentation to use with Jehovah's Witnesses, Mormons, and others who deny the full deity of Jesus Christ.

"The First and the Last" Presentation

I title this section on the deity of Christ "The First and the Last" not only because the presentation uses this term, but also because it uses the first and last chapters of Revelation to prove the point. We begin by reading Revelation 1:8: "'I am the *Alpha and the Omega*' says the *Lord God*, 'who is and who was and who is to come, the *Almighty*'" (emphasis added). This Scripture teaches us a few points: The "Alpha and Omega" is the "Lord God Almighty," and He is coming.

All will agree, but the Jehovah's Witnesses will point out that their bible inserts "Jehovah" for "Lord." Refer them to their *Kingdom Interlinear Translation* so they can see for themselves that "Jehovah" is not in the Greek text but is an insertion by the "translators" of their bible. In spite of this, all can agree that Almighty God calls Himself "the Alpha and the Omega."

Turn now to Revelation 22. There are several speakers in this chapter, but we want to single out the "Alpha and Omega" speaker to see what else He has to say. Insist on reading the verses *in context*. The speaker does not change between verses 12 through 16, so let's consider Revelation 22:12-16:

> "Behold, I am coming quickly, and My reward is with Me, to render to every man according to what he has done. I am the *Alpha and the Omega, the first and the last*, the beginning and the end." Blessed are those who wash their robes, that they may have the right to the tree of life, and may enter by the gates into the city. Outside are the dogs and the sorcerers and the immoral persons and the murderers and the idolaters, and everyone who loves and practices lying. "*I, Jesus*, have sent My angel to testify to you these things for the churches. I am the root and the offspring of David, the bright morning star" (emphasis added).

Only now, with verse 17, does the speaker change. Therefore the same speaker, namely the Alpha and Omega, has said all the above things. He is "coming quickly" (agreeing with Revelation 1:8 that we've already noted), He is the "Alpha and the Omega," He is the "first and the last," and

He identifies Himself as "I, Jesus." The apostle John evidently agrees for in verse 20 he records, "He who testifies to these things says, 'Yes, I am coming quickly.' Amen. Come, Lord Jesus."

Jehovah's Witnesses will become agitated at this point, insisting that verse 12 is probably Jesus, then verse 13 must be Jehovah, then verse 16 is Jesus again. Rather than arguing, ask them, "Do you agree that in verse 13 the "Alpha and Omega" calls Himself "the first and the last"? They must agree. Remark that Revelation 1 leaves us in no doubt as to the identity of "the first and the last." Turn to Revelation 1:13-18. This account is a vision of the "son of man." Ask them who this is. They will reply, "Jesus." You will agree. You could take the time to read through the vision, but concentrate on verses 17 and 18, where the apostle John says:

> And when I saw Him, I fell at His feet as a dead man. And He laid His right hand upon me, saying, "Do not be afraid; *I am the first and the last*, and the living One, and *I was dead*, and behold, I am alive forevermore, and I have the keys of death and of Hades" (emphasis added).

Jesus has here called Himself "the first and the last"— the same as He did in Revelation 22:13 where He also called Himself the "Alpha and the Omega." It is obviously Jesus speaking also in Revelation 1:8, where He repeats that He is "coming," He is the "Alpha and the Omega," and He is "Almighty God." We'll read Revelation 1:8 again to fully establish the claims of Jesus Christ: " 'I am the Alpha and the Omega,' says the Lord God [Jesus Christ], 'who is and who was and who is to come, the Almighty.' "

Jesus Christ is truly Almighty God by His own witness of the fact. Therefore, He is not some secondary god, nor one god among many, nor the Archangel Michael, nor only a good man. Jesus Christ is Almighty God manifest in the flesh.

What About the Ho Theos Argument?

Ho Theos means "the God" in Greek, and Jehovah's Witnesses claim this can only be Jehovah God. We therefore refer them to the following Scriptures and ask them to check them out in their *Kingdom Interlinear Translation*. In each case Jesus Christ is called *Ho Theos*, "the God."

> Prophecy called Jesus "the God" (Matthew 1:23).
>
> The disciples called Jesus "the God" (John 20:25-28).
>
> The Father called Jesus "the God" (Hebrews 1:8).

Jesus Is "The God With Us"

Jesus Christ is Almighty God (Revelation 1:8), the God (Scriptures above), the true God (1 John 5:20), and finally the only God. First Timothy 1:16,17 reads,

> And yet for this reason I found mercy, in order that in me as the foremost, Jesus Christ might demonstrate His perfect patience, as an example for those who would believe in Him for eternal life. Now to the King eternal, immortal, invisible, the only God, be honor and glory forever and ever, Amen.

Yes, Jesus Christ is eternal (not created, as Jehovah's Witnesses teach), and He is called "the only God." Point out the location of the "Amen" in these Scriptures. Jehovah's Witnesses would like verse 16 to be Jesus, but verse 17 to be Jehovah. That's not possible. There were no chapter and verse divisions in the early manuscripts, and the "Amen" closes the thought. Furthermore, the subject is Jesus Christ.

There is only one true God in Scripture. He has revealed Himself in the person of the Father and in the person of the Son, Jesus Christ. He has also revealed Himself in the person of the Holy Spirit, but we are not dealing with that subject at this time, but with the deity of Jesus Christ.

Understanding Jesus' Humanity As Well As His Deity

Jesus is truly God, but He is also truly man. It is the Scriptures dealing with His humanity that cause the most distortions in the cult doctrines. Therefore, let's understand them and be ready to explain them in context.

John 1:14 says, "And the Word became flesh, and dwelt among us." Yes, the Word who was God came down to this earth. Why? And for how long? Hebrews 2:9 answers,

> But we do see Him who has been made for a little while lower than the angels, namely, Jesus, because of the suffering of death crowned with glory and honor, that by the grace of God He might taste death for everyone.

So this humanity, this humility of Jesus, was to be "for a little while," and He would "taste death for everyone."

Jesus' Humanity Explained in Philippians

Verses 5 and 6 of Philippians 2 begin regarding the humanity of Jesus, "Have this attitude in yourselves which was also in Christ Jesus, who, although He existed in the form of God, did not regard equality with God a thing to be grasped." The phrase "existed in the form of God" means literally in the Greek that He "never ceased being in the form of God." Remembering this point, we continue to the phrase, "[He] did not regard equality with God a thing to be grasped."

The cults love to disregard the first phrase and seize on the second to try to "prove" Jesus inferior. However, in context, Jesus Christ never ceased being God, but rather than grasping after the equality that was His, He chose a course of humanity and humility. Joseph H. Thayer, D.D., in his *A Greek-English Lexicon* gives the English translation as "retained" rather than "grasped." This makes the meaning even clearer. Rather than "retaining" His equality, Jesus emptied Himself of it in order to function as a man. Verses 7 and 8 of Philippians 2 continue on,

> But emptied Himself, taking the form of a bond-servant, and being made in the likeness of men. And being found in appearance as a man. He humbled Himself by becoming obedient to the point of death, even death on a cross.

As a Man, Did Jesus Lose His Deity?

The answer to the above question is "Never!" Jesus Christ was not just a good man as some cults teach; He was God manifest in the flesh. He did function totally as a man while on earth, but He was always God. Colossians 2:8,9 warns that false teachers will deceive people on this very point, as do the Jehovah's Witnesses.

> See to it that no one takes you captive through philosophy and empty deception, according to the tradition of men, according to the elementary principles of the world, rather than according to Christ. For in *Him all the fulness of Deity dwells in bodily form* (emphasis added).

All is all, and full is full, and "all the fulness of Deity" (Godhead, Godship) is dwelling in Christ *"in the flesh."*

Why Did Jesus Become a Man?

This was the only way mankind could be redeemed, because of God's perfect justice. Remember how under the Old Law Covenant it was "an eye for an eye" and "a tooth for a tooth"? So also, since Adam—a perfect man—lost eternal life for us, Jesus Christ—a perfect man—could redeem it back. Romans 5:12,15 explains:

> Therefore, just as through one man sin entered into the world, and death through sin, and so death spread to all men, because all sinned... but the free gift is not like the transgression. For if by the transgression of the one the many died, much more did the grace of God and the gift by the grace of the one Man, Jesus Christ, abound to the many.

Truly, Jesus Christ, "God with us," did function as a man on earth. He performed His miracles in the power of the Holy Spirit, and promised His disciples, "The works that I do shall he do also; and greater works than these shall he do" (John 14:12). The disciples were mere men empowered by the Holy Spirit, and yet were promised that they could carry on as Jesus did. Jesus truly functioned as a man while on earth, fulfilling all the requirements to redeem us from Adam's sin.

Did Jesus Ever Say He Was Inferior to the Father?

The cult groups denying the deity of Jesus Christ always use Scriptures from the time of His humanity and try to apply them to His deity. A favorite example is John 14:28, quoting Jesus, "The Father is greater than I."

Is Jesus saying He is inferior to the Father? No, if Jesus wanted to say He was inferior, He would have said, "The Father is *better* than I." The Greek word for "better" means "higher in nature." Jesus did not use that word, since He is not inferior or lower in nature than the Father, as the cults teach. Jesus used the Greek word for "greater," which means "higher in position." While Jesus was humbled, emptied, functioning as a man, the Father was in a higher position. This would be much like the president and vice-president of a company. The president is in a higher position than the vice-president, but by nature they are both men and equal.

At this point the Jehovah's Witnesses will probably ask how Jesus could be on earth as "God with us," and the Father could be in heaven, also as God. Jesus even prayed to the Father while on earth. The answer is found in Isaiah 55:9: "For as the heavens are higher than the earth, so are My ways higher than your ways, and My thoughts than your thoughts." Luke 1:37 agrees, "For nothing will be impossible with God."

We should never try to limit God to our human under-standing. If God chooses to be manifest on earth as Jesus Christ and at the same time be in heaven as the Father, He can do anything He wants to do! "God is spirit..." (John 4:24) and does not have our limitations.

Jesus' Claims While on Earth

> For this cause therefore the Jews were seeking all the more to kill Him, because He not only was breaking the Sabbath, but also was calling God His own Father, *making Himself equal with God* (John 5:18, emphasis added).

> "I and the Father are one." The Jews took up stones again to stone Him. Jesus answered them, "I showed you many good works from the Father; for which of them are you stoning Me?" The Jews answered Him, "For a good work we do not stone You, but for blasphemy; and because You, being a man, make *Yourself out to be God*" (John 10:30-33, emphasis added).

If Jesus had been claiming to be only "a god" as Jehovah's Witnesses and others teach, then He would not have been charged with "blasphemy." Jesus knew He was God, His disciples worshiped Him, eyewitnesses testified to His claims to be God, and the whole church believed Acts 20:28, which tells the elders, "Be on guard for yourselves and for all the flock, among which the Holy Spirit has made you overseers, to shepherd the church of God, which He purchased with His own blood."

While He was on earth, Jesus was subject (not inferior) to His heavenly Father, and this subjection or submission appears to continue until the full establishment of the new heavens and new earth. Subject—yes, inferior—no!

Jesus Calls Himself the "I Am"

In the gospel of John, chapter 8, we find Jesus disputing with the religious leaders. He spoke of knowing Abraham.

> The Jews therefore said to Him, "You are not yet fifty years old, and have You seen Abraham?" Jesus said to them, "Truly, truly, I say to you, before Abraham was born, I AM." Therefore they picked up stones to throw at Him; but Jesus hid Himself, and went out of the temple (John 8:57-59).

Why were the Jews so angry and ready to stone Jesus? It was because He took the memorial name of God to all generations and applied it to Himself. Those Jews knew very well the account in Exodus 3 where Moses was about to go in before Pharaoh and was in dialogue with God.

> Then Moses said to God, "Behold, I am going to the sons of Israel, and I shall say to them, 'The God of your fathers has sent me to you.' Now they may say to me, 'What is His name?' What shall I say to them?" And God said to Moses, "I AM WHO I AM"; and He said, "Thus you shall say to the sons of Israel, 'I AM has sent me to you'" (Exodus 3:13,14).

Here we find a plain answer to a plain question. Moses asked God's name, and God said it was "I AM." God then went on to reveal a second name, "YHWH." He concluded the giving of both names by saying, "This is My name forever, and this is My memorial-name to all generations" (Exodus 3:15).

Jesus used the first-revealed name in John 8:58, declaring that He was the "I AM." How important is it that we believe Jesus' statement concerning His identity? John 8:24 in the original Greek tells us, "I said therefore to you, that you shall die in your sins; for *unless you believe that I am,* you shall die in your sins" (emphasis added).

We must believe that Jesus is the "I AM" or deity, or we will die in our sins, without salvation. The leaders of the Jehovah's Witnesses have extensively distorted their Bible in these key areas. Please refer to chapter 2 for details. It is vitally important that Christians be able to defend the deity of Jesus Christ to the cults.

The Faithful Finish of Jesus' Earthly Life

> Therefore also God highly exalted Him, and bestowed on Him the name which is above every name, that at the name of Jesus every knee should bow, of those who are in heaven, and on earth, and under the earth, and that every tongue should confess that Jesus Christ is Lord, to the glory of God the Father (Philippians 2:9-11).

Yes, Jesus is exalted in the heavens, having perfectly redeemed us. In three worlds—in heaven, on earth, and under the earth—every knee *shall bow* in worship to Jesus Christ. I tell the Jehovah's Witnesses they can either worship Jesus now *willingly* in the day of salvation or they will worship him *unwillingly* in the day of judgment. Do not refuse Jesus the worship He is due as God.

In Conclusion

We need to rise to the defense of our Lord and Savior, Jesus Christ, who is truly God and truly man. We need to tell the cults with the authority of God's Word behind us that Jesus Christ is not any kind of a "secondary god," or the "archangel Michael," or "merely a good man." Jesus Christ is the *only* mediator between God and man. We close with Acts 4:12: "And there is salvation in no one else; for there is no other name under heaven that has been given among men, by which we must be saved."

The Deity of Jesus Christ

Scripture Context	Applied to the Father Jehovah	Applied to Son Jesus
Both "God"	Psalm 89:26	Hebrews 1:8
Both "Mighty God"	Jeremiah 32:18	Isaiah 9:6
Both "True God"	Jeremiah 10:10	1 John 5:20
"Almighty God"	Genesis 17:1	Revelation 1:8 with 22:20
Both "Only God"	Isaiah 45:22	1 Timothy 1:16,17
"Lord of Lords"	Deuteronomy 10:17	Revelation 17:14
"Lord of Glory"	Psalm 24:10	1 Corinthians 2:8
"Holy, Holy, Holy"	Isaiah 6:3	Revelation 4:8 with 22:20
Both "Holy One"	Isaiah 12:6	Acts 3:14
Both "I AM"	Exodus 3:14	John 8:58
"Alpha and Omega"	Revelation 1:8	Revelation 22:13-16
Both "Creator"	Isaiah 44:24	Colossians 1:16
Both "Savior"	Isaiah 43:11	Luke 2:11
Both "King"	Psalm 29:10	Revelation 17:14
"Redeemed a People"	2 Samuel 7:23,24	Titus 2:14
Both "Father"	Matthew 6:9	Isaiah 9:6
Both "Rock"	Deuteronomy 32:4	1 Corinthians 10:4
Both "Judge"	Genesis 18:25	2 Timothy 4:8
Both "Shepherd"	Psalm 23:1	John 10:2
Both "Same"	Malachi 3:6	Hebrews 1:12; 13:8
"First and Last"	Isaiah 44:6	Revelation 1:17
Both "Above All"	Psalm 97:9	John 3:31
Both "Over All"	Psalm 103:19	Romans 9:5
Both "Worshiped"	Psalm 95:6	Matthew 28:9
"Control the Elements"	Psalm 107:29	Matthew 8:27
No End to Years	Psalm 102:25-27	Hebrews 1:10-12
Everlasting Throne	Psalm 93:2	Hebrews 1:8
Endless Kingdom	Psalm 146:10	2 Peter 1:11
Both Exalted	Psalm 108:5	Philippians 2:9
Both "Pierced"	Zechariah 12:10	Revelation 1:7
Both Valued and Sold for 30 Pieces of Silver	Zechariah 11:12,13	Matthew 26:14-16

Truly, God's blood purchased the church (Acts 20:28).

Chapter 10

WITNESSING EFFECTIVELY TO THE CULTS

This chapter is written with years of experience as our best teacher. We are always learning, of course, but we want to share with you what we have found to be the most effective methods of winning souls out of the cults.

An Early Lesson Learned

When I was set free from Jehovah's Witness doctrine after 15 years and had "deprogrammed" myself by intense study of the Word, I was in a unique position to set Jehovah's Witnesses straight. I soon found out I was winning every argument, but I wasn't winning souls for Christ. Finally, I fell on my knees and cried out to the Lord to show me how to win souls and not just arguments.

Through the patient leading of the Holy Spirit and the Word of God, I was taught these important Scriptural steps to set people free from cults. It works because it is God's way, not man's way. The beginning steps may seem elementary to some, but we are constantly faced with frantic family members who have a loved one in a cult, and they have little or no foundation in true Christianity.

1. Recognize That You Need Help!

Recognize that you cannot proceed on your own strength but you can do all things in Christ's strength. Philippians 4:13 says, "I can do all things through Him who strengthens me."

You must be "born again" to proceed. Take your Bible and read John 3:1-7. Verse 7 reads, "Do not marvel that I said to you, 'You must be born again.'" If this was a requirement for the righteous, religious Nicodemus, who was a community leader, it is a requirement for all who need help in spiritual matters.

If you are not sure you have had this experience of being "born again" or "saved," avail yourself of this free gift from God. Ephesians 2:8,9, says, "For by grace you have been saved through faith; and that not of yourselves, it is the gift of God; not as a result of works, that no one should boast."

Repent or turn around. Acts 3:19,20 says, "Repent therefore and return, that your sins may be wiped away, in order that times of refreshing may come from the presence of the Lord; and that He may send Jesus, the Christ appointed for you."

Confess Christ and believe. Romans 10:9,10 says,

> That if you confess with your mouth Jesus as Lord, and believe in your heart that God raised Him from the dead, you shall be saved; for with the heart man believes, resulting in righteousness, and with the mouth he confesses, resulting in salvation.

Receive Christ by praying and asking Him to come into your life as your Savior and Lord. John 1:12,13 makes this promise,

> But as many as received Him, to them He gave the right to become children of God, even to those who believe in His name, who were born not of blood, nor of the will of the flesh, nor of the will of man, but of God.

You must have the help of the Holy Spirit in your Christian walk as well. This is also a free gift, and you should ask God to give you the Holy Spirit to help you. Luke 11:13 says, "How much more shall your heavenly Father give the Holy Spirit to those who ask Him."

Without the saving grace of the Lord Jesus, and the gift of the Holy Spirit, we would be operating without power. We would be trying to fight spiritual battles with fleshly weapons. Make no mistake: You will need God's power in your life to set the cultist free.

2. Be Prepared for Battle

All the parts of step one are necessary because you will find yourself in a spiritual battle for the cultist's soul. You must fight spiritually. Take your Bible and read Ephesians 6:10-18, which will show you how to put on the "full armor of God" so you will be ready for this battle. Verse 10 begins by saying, "Finally, be strong in the Lord, and in the strength of His might." Learn to use the Lord's strength, and not your own.

Deal with any fear you may feel. Fear comes from two sources: our own flesh, and the enemy, Satan. Remember that any fear you feel does not come from God. Second Timothy 1:7 (KJV) says, "For God hath not given us the spirit of fear; but of power, and of love, and of a sound mind."

Recognize that Satan has no power over one who is washed in the blood of Jesus Christ. First John 3:8 says, "The Son of God appeared for this purpose, that He might destroy the works of the devil." First John 4:4 tells us, "You are from God, little children, and have overcome them; because greater is He who is in you than he who is in the world." First John 5:18 further tells us that "the evil one does not touch him." This is speaking of the person "born of God."

I am always amazed to meet Christians who are in fear of Satan, believing that he can even "read their minds" or "put thoughts in their heads." What nonsense! God alone knows our minds and hearts, according to Scripture. The only power Satan can have over us is what we give him by our mental assent, even as Eve did. We are sanctified spirit, soul, and body, according to 1 Thessalonians 5:23, which reads, "Now may the God of peace Himself sanctify you entirely; and may your spirit and soul and body be preserved complete, without blame at the coming of our Lord Jesus Christ." Christians are "overcomers in Christ," and as such should not fear the devil or any man.

3. Learn the Power of Prayer

The longer we are involved in helping people come out of the cults, the more we have learned to rely on the Holy Spirit to convict them and set them free. Intercessory prayer not only sets the captives free, but strengthens your own Christian convictions. Avail yourself of the power that is given to the believer who earnestly prays. "If you abide in Me, and My words abide in you, ask whatever you wish, and it shall be done for you" (John 15:7).

4. Develop Confidence in the Word of God

Begin locating and reading suitable Scriptures which will strengthen your faith. I believe in following the example of Jesus Christ, who quoted Scriptures out loud in Satan's hearing (see Matthew 4:1-11). There are many Scriptures that will strengthen your faith, such as Acts 16:31: "Believe in the Lord Jesus, and you shall be saved, you and your household." First John 5:14,15 says,

> And this is the confidence which we have before Him, that, if we ask anything according to His will, He hears us. And if we know that He hears us in whatever we ask, we know that we have the requests which we have asked from Him.

5. Prepare to Set Matters Straight with the Word of God

Realize that the Bible is not just words on paper, but is alive and powerful.

> For the word of God is living and active and sharper than any two-edged sword, and piercing as far as the division of soul and spirit, of both joints and marrow, and able to judge the thoughts and intentions of the heart (Hebrews 4:12).

Learn Scriptures that prove the error of the particular cult, and be prepared to share these with the cultists from your Bible.

> All Scripture is inspired by God and profitable for teaching, for reproof, for correction, for training in righteousness; that the man of God may be

adequate, equipped for every good work (2 Timothy 3:16,17).

6. *Power-Filled Praying*

Before entering into any discussions with a cultist or sharing Scripture with him, you need to pray with authority. It is sometimes good to have another strong believer with you and pray in agreement as Matthew 18:19,20 says,

> Again I say to you, that if two of you agree on earth about anything that they may ask, it shall be done for them by My Father who is in heaven. For where two or three have gathered together in My name, there I am in their midst.

It is good to name the person you are praying for and ask the Lord to convict him of his error. Ask for the anointing of the Holy Spirit for the encounter, and be assured that Christ is in your midst as promised. People in cults are under a spirit of deception, and your words will not penetrate without this divine help, no matter how well-prepared you are.

Don't despair if results don't appear immediately. God's Word cannot go out and return without producing results. Isaiah 55:11 says, "So shall My word be which goes forth from My mouth; it shall not return to Me empty, without accomplishing what I desire, and without succeeding in the matter for which I sent it."

Be assured that the Word of God will begin working in the cultist, convicting him of his error, even if it doesn't look like it on the surface. Don't try and do the work of the Holy Spirit. It is your job to witness for Christ, and it is the work of the Holy Spirit to convict people. This takes time. God's timing is not your timing.

7. *The Waiting Game—Exercise Time for Your Faith*

While waiting for the promised results, your faith must go into action. You must learn to walk by faith. Second Corinthians 5:7 says, "For we walk by faith, not by sight." Never be discouraged by the circumstances or let your emotions rule you. Faithfully continue in intercessory prayer, Bible reading, and learning the Scriptures. Believe that God will reward you for your faith in Him.

> Now faith is the assurance of things hoped for, the conviction of things not seen.... And without faith it is impossible to please Him, for he who comes to God must believe that He is, and that He is a rewarder of those who seek Him (Hebrews 11:1,6).

Methods We Use to Reach Cults for Christ

First off, we cannot employ any of these methods without the cooperation of the body of Christ universal. We are here to help each other, and are in this outreach together.

1. *Seminar Teachings, Films, and Videos.* This is a training program for the body of Christ, who, in turn, will be prepared to witness for Christ to the cults at their doors. The chapters of this book are typical seminars in print. We also have films, videos, and slide presentations to train Christians how to witness. Your church library should have an assortment of these videos.

2. *Direct Mail Outreach.* We ask Christians to send in to us the names and addresses of persons they know who are involved in the cults. We then do an "anonymous" mailing

of Christian literature designed especially for the cultist. We offer to enter into correspondence with them, and many write back. We never reveal the source of their name. The cultist receives the mail in the privacy of his own home, free from the prying eyes of the elders, and can peruse it in secret. It has been the first step to freedom for many trapped in the cults.

3. *Neighborhood Concern.* In this outreach, we ask all Christians to take responsibility for their own neighborhoods. That means watching your neighborhood and noting which neighbors are inviting the cults in or talking to them at their door. These neighbors are *in crisis* and are seeking for God. Something has happened to them to make them vulnerable, such as a death, a marriage breakdown, or rebellious children. They are looking for answers. Arm yourself with some appropriate tracts and go over for a visit. Many are led to Christ on the first call. Take your pastor or a Christian friend if you are nervous, but go! At the very least, send in their address so we can mail some literature to help them.

4. *In-Home Return Visit Training.* For this outreach we ask that in each church one person or couple will take the responsibility and "study up" on the Jehovah's Witnesses and Mormons. It is not as difficult as you think. We have literature and tapes available that will provide all the training you need. You then become the pastor's helper in the area of the cults. Persons in your congregation can invite the cult members at their doors to come back at a later time when you can be there also. This accomplishes two things. The householder receives "on-the-spot" training, and the cultists receive a good witness for Christ.

Remember, it is not your ability so much as your availability. This could be your missionary service to our Lord. Workers are needed in this specialized field. Those interested in this outreach should read our book *What You Need to Know About Jehovah's Witnesses* for practical help to get started.

Some may wish to go one step further and take teaching videos around to the various study groups and church meetings in your area. MacGregor Ministries provides literature at discounted rates if you wish to step out in this ministry.

5. *Tracting Your Area*. We have available two excellent warning tracts about the Jehovah's Witnesses and Mormons. Many churches have distributed these in their areas, along with a salvation tract or an invitation to attend church. This "net" usually brings those studying with the cults into the true fold.

Some churches have printed up stickers that say "No Visits by Jehovah's Witnesses or Mormons Please" and offered these free to families in their neighborhoods. This is a form of protection for non-Christian families, but Christians should be witnessing to those at their doors, not turning them away.

In Conclusion

We are committed to reaching out with the love of Christ to those in the cults. We take very seriously the Scripture in 2 Timothy 2:24-26,

> And the Lord's bond-servant must not be quarrelsome, but be kind to all, able to teach, patient when wronged, with gentleness correcting those

who are in opposition, if perhaps God may grant them repentance leading to the knowledge of the truth, and they may come to their senses and escape from the snare of the devil, having been held captive by him to do his will.

The whole purpose of this book and of our ministry is to reach out with the love of Christ to those trapped in the counterfeits of Christianity and to introduce them to the real Jesus Christ. We hope you feel the same way after reading this book. May you be blessed as you witness for Christ and set the captives free.

WHAT DO THEY THINK OF CHRIST?

Adelphi Organization—New Age view of Christ.

Advanced Organization of Los Angeles (AOLA)—Uses philosophy and Scientology.

Aetherius Society—UFO group receives messages from "Master Jesus" in outer space.

Ahmadiyya Movement—Islam; Jesus a prophet only.

Alamo Christian Foundation—Correct doctrine on Jesus but cultish in their denunciation of other Christians.

Aletheia Psycho-Physical Foundation—New Age view of Christ.

Alphabiotic New Life Center—New Age view of Christ; Yoga.

Ambassadors for Christ—Denies deity of Christ; similar to Jehovah's Witnesses.

American Babaji Yoga Sangam—Hinduism; Yoga.

American Imagery Institute—New Age view of Christ.

American Leadership College Inc.—New Age/occult view of Christ.

AMORC—See "Rosicrucianism."

Ananda Marga Yoga Society—Founder Maha-Guru is an incarnation of God.

Ancient Wisdom Connection—Lord Sananda is incarnation of Christ.

Andean Explorers Foundation—See "Jamilians."

Anthroposophical Society—Jesus just man until age 30, and then received "Christ Essence."

Apostolic Overcoming Holy Church of God—Modalistic view of Christ.

Aquarian Church of Universal Service—Similar to Unitarian-Universalist; denies deity of Christ.

Aquarian Perspective Interplanetary Mission—Receives messages from UFOs.

Arete Truth Center—New Age view of Christ.

Arica Institute Inc.—"Christ cannot be God."

Arizona Metaphysical Society—New Age view of Christ.

Arm of the Lord—To invite Jesus into one's life is "satanic."

Armageddon Time Ark Base Operation—UFO group.

Armstrongism—See "Worldwide Church of God" and the "Church of God International," as well as other offshoot groups in list.

Arunachala Ashram—Hinduism; also called Maharishi Center.

Ascended Master Teaching Foundation—Believes each one can be "I AM," not just Jesus.

Ascent Foundation—New Age view of Christ; similar to est, Lifespring, and Silva Mind Control.

Assemblies of the Called Out Ones of "Yah"—Denies Trinity.

Assemblies of Yahweh—Denies Trinity.

Association for Christian Development—Splinter group of Worldwide Church of God.

Association for Past-Life Research and Therapies, Inc.—New Age view of Christ; astrology.

Association for Research and Enlightenment (Edgar Cayce)—A portion of God called Soul reincarnated eventually as Christ.

Association Sananda & Sanat Kumara, Inc.—"Christ consciousness"; New Age.

Astara—Speaks of "Cosmic Christ"; denies His eternal nature.

Astro Computing Services—Astrology and horoscopes; New Age view of Christ.

Aum Center—Believes man is God; New Age.

Author Services, Inc.—Promotes Scientology.

Avatar—New Age view of Christ; similar to est, Lifespring.

Awareness Research Foundation, Inc.—UFOs; ESP, etc.

Baba Ram Dass (Hanuman Foundation)—Disciples encouraged to acknowledge their inner divinity and oneness with universal deity; Hinduistic.

The Baha'i Faith—Christ one of the nine great manifestations of divinity; Baha'u'llah greater.

Bawa Muhaiyaddeen Fellowship—Man becomes God.

Bhagwan Shree Rajneesh—See "Rajneesh Meditation Centers."

Bible Believers Inc.—Promotes Branhamism.

Bible Speaks—Noted for shepherding and control of followers.

Bible Students—Splinter groups of Jehovah's Witnesses; deny deity of Christ.

Bible Studies Fellowship—Splinter group of Jehovah's Witnesses; deny deity of Christ.

Bible Way Publications—Splinter group of Jehovah's Witnesses; deny deity of Christ.

Black Muslim—Jesus was black and only a prophet; Allah incarnate is Wallace Ford.

Bookmark—Splinter group of Christian Science.

Branhamism—William Branham; denies Trinity.

Brandlen Institute—New Age view of Christ.

Brother Julius—Believes he is incarnation of Jesus.

Brotherhood of Eternal Truth—Astrology; spiritualistic.

Brotherhood of the White Temple Inc.—New Age/occult.

Bubba Free John (Dawn Horse Fellowship; Free Primative Church of Divine Communion; Free Community Order; Laughing Man Inst.)—Claims he (Franklin Jones) is incarnation of God, a guru to be worshiped, equal with Christ.

Buddha's Universal Church—Similar to Buddhism.

Buddhism—Christ not recognized as deity. Zen Buddhism also does not affirm the existence of the living God.

Builders—Views God as Father/Mother; Christ-consciousness.

Builders of the Adytum Ltd.—Occult.

Cabala (Kabbalah)—Doctrine of deity recognizes only two deities: the hidden god or the infinite great divine Nothing, and the dynamic god of religious experience; mystical.

Carp—See "Unification Church."

Causa—See "Unification Church."

Center for Spiritual Awareness (Christian Spiritual Alliance)—Jesus a man who reached "Christ-consciousness."

Chakras—Type of Yoga.

Children of God (Family of Love)—Began fundamentalist but degenerated into occult.

Choosing the Light, Inc.—New Age view of Christ.

Christ Family—Lightening Amen claims he is incarnation of Christ.

Christ Light Community—See "New Age Church of Truth."

Christadelphians—Jesus did not exist before birth to Mary; not God.

Christian Community—Similar to Anthroposophical Society.

Christian Millenial Fellowship—Splinter group of Jehovah's Witnesses; denies deity of Jesus.

Christian Renewal Ministry—Splinter group of Jehovah's Witnesses.

Christian Science—Christ is a Divine idea and His blood doesn't cleanse us.

Church for Positive Living—New Age; Native Indian folklore.

Church of All Worlds—Occult and pagan.

Church of Armageddon (Love Family)—Follow prophet "Love Israel"; use Yoga and drugs.

Church of Bible Understanding (Forever Family)—Founder Traill is one true access to Bible understanding; denies Trinity.

Church of Christ—Most believe baptism necessary for salvation.

Church of Christ, Scientist—See "Christian Science."

Church of Christ, Temple Lot—Splinter group of Mormons.

Church of Christ with the Elijah Message—Splinter group of Mormons.

Church of Cosmic Origin—New Age view of Christ.

Church of Divine Influence—Impersonal god-force.

Church of God Evangelistic—Splinter group of Worldwide Church of God.

Church of God, Faith of Abraham—Splinter group of Jehovah's Witnesses; deny Trinity.

Church of God General Conference—Deny Trinity.

Church of God International—Splinter of Worldwide Church of God headed by Garner Ted Armstrong; denies Trinity.

Church of God, Seventh Day—Baptism necessary for salvation.

Church of God (7th Day)—Denies Trinity.

Church of God, the Eternal—Similar to Worldwide Church of God; denies Trinity.

Church of Hakeem—"god within" makes people rich.

Church of Illumination—New Age; similar to Rosicrucians.

Church of Jesus Christ of Latter-day Saints (Mormons)—Jesus was the spirit-brother of Lucifer, born on earth by the Father's sexual relations with the virgin Mary; Jesus "a god."

Church of Jesus Power—Astral projection.

Church of Light—New Age view of Christ.

Church of the Living Word (The Walk)—Followers become the Living Word (Christ) to the world.

Church of Metaphysical Christianity—Jesus an ascended master.

Church of Perfect Liberty—Man is a manifestation of God.

Church of Satan—Occult.

Church of Scientology—See "Scientology."

Church of the Final Judgement—See "Process Church of the Final Judgement."

Church of the Most High God—Holy Spirit is God the Mother.

Church of the Most High Goddess—Revival of Egyptian goddess religion.

Church of the Movement of Spiritual Inner Awareness—New Age view of Christ.

Church of the New Birth—New Age/occult.

Church of the New Jerusalem—See "Swedenborg Foundation."

Church of the Tree of Life—Anything goes that's legal.

Church of the Trinity—New Age view of Jesus.

Church Universal and Triumphant (Summit Int.; Summit Lighthouse)—Jesus a man with Christ-consciousness within Him. Similar to "I AM."

Circle of Light—New Age view of Christ.

Community of Jesus—Controversial commune; reports of mind control and excessive shepherding.

Concept Therapy—New Age view of Christ.

Conciliation Ministries—Conversation should be to inner self, not to Jesus.

Confraternity of Deists—Reject concept of a Savior.

Consciousness Connection—New Age view of Jesus.

Cooneyites (Two by Twos)—Jesus inherited Adam's fallen sin nature and did not finish His earthly mission, but they are doing so.

Cosmerism—Mixes Christianity and Buddhism; all religions have truth.

Cosmic Awareness Communications—New Age view of Christ; "Force" also spoke through Krishna and Edgar Cayce.

Cosmic Communication Commune—Believes in "Cosmic Spirit."

Cosmic Science Research Foundation—New Age concepts.

Course in Miracles—All is illusion; man is still in heaven.

Coven Gardens—Occult/pagan.

Creation Calendar—Keeping law necessary for salvation.

Crystal Consciousness—New Age view of Christ.

Dawn Bible Students Assoc. (Frank and Earnest)—Jesus created, not God; deny Trinity.

Dhyana-ma-ndiram—Jesus one of many reincarnations of God.

Dianetics—See "Scientology."

Discover Seminars—New Age concepts.

Divine Light Center—Hinduism; voodoo, etc.

Divine Light Mission of Guru Maharaj Ji—Followers believe their guru is Christ come again.

Divine Science—Similar to Christian Science.

Divine Science of Light and Sound—New Age concepts.

Divine Word Foundation—New Age; separate Jesus and Christ.

Dungeons and Dragons—Occult board game.

Eckankar (The Ancient Art of Soul-Travel)—Christ is "god as all men are god."

Ecstasy—New Age; man is God; hedonistic.

Emissaries of Divine Light (Ontologists)—Does not accept the atoning work of Christ; mystical.

Epiphany Bible Students Association—Splinter group of Laymen's Home Missionary Movement from Jehovah's Witnesses.

Esalen Institute—"Human Potential" movement; mystical.

Essene Gospel of Peace—New Age; "Jesus" channels.

Essene Light Center—Belief in ascended beings; Father/ Mother God.

est (Erhard Seminars Training; The Forum)—Teaches that each person is a god himself.

Eternal Flame—Chas. Paul Brown, the leader, claims to be the very body and blood of Christ.

Faithbuilders Fellowship—Denies deity of Jesus.

Family of Love—See "Children of God."

The Farm—Jesus was a man indwelt by Christ- consciousness.

Fellowship for Spiritual Understanding—Man is God.

Fellowship of the Inner Light—Man can become Creator.

Fifth Epocal Fellowship—Splinter group of Urantia.

Findhorn Foundation University of Light—Separates Jesus and Christ; appear to be pantheistic and believe in plant spirits.

First Temple of the Craft of W.I.C.A.—Witchcraft.

First Universal Church of God-Realization—New Age.

First World Conclave of Light—See "Unarius Academy of Science."

Flag Service Organization—See "Scientology."

Forever Family—See "Church of Bible Understanding."

The Forum—See "est."

Foundation Church of the New Birth—Man becomes very essence of God.

Foundation Faith of God—See "Process, Church of the Final Judgement."

The Foundation Faith of the Millennium—Denies deity of Christ; only a prophet.

Foundation for Higher Spiritual Learning—"I AM" philosophy, taking attributes of God to self.

Foundation for Inner Peace—See "Course in Miracles."

Foundation for Shamanic Studies—Occult.

Foundation for Unlimited Consciousness—New Age view of Christ.

Foundation of Human Understanding (Roy Masters)—Neglects Christ or mentions Him in a negative context.

Frank and Earnest—See "Dawn Bible Students Assoc."

Free Masonry—Jesus a man like us.

Freewinds Relay Office—Promotes Scientology.

G.A.P. Ministries—Keeps old law.

Gateways Institute—New Age view of Christ.

Global Family—All is God.

God's House of Prayer—Keeping old law necessary for salvation.

Golden Dawn—Occult/magic.

Grail Foundation of America—Esoteric teachings; discount some of Christ's teachings.

Great White Brotherhood—Group of ascended masters; usually includes name of Jesus.

Greater Grace World Outreach—See "Bible Speaks."

Guild for Hermetic Revelation—New Age/astrology.

Hare Krishna (ISKCON)—Jesus one of their gurus, but Hare Krishna is their God.

Health Conscious Services—Each person is own master.

Heaven's Magic—See "Children of God."

High Point—New Age view of Christ.

Himalayan International Institute of Yoga Science and Philosophy—Christ-consciousness view.

Hinduism—No need of a personal Savior; each one attains to becoming "a god" or attaining "cosmic consciousness."

Holm Community—Seeks divine evolution.

Holy Grail Foundation—New Age views.

The Holy Order of Mans—Jesus a man indwelt by Christ-consciousness.

Holy Shankaracharya Order—Hindu theology.

Holy Spirit Assoc. for the Unification of World Christianity—See "Unification Church."

House of Prayer for All People—Believes in Atlantis.

House of Yahweh—See "Yahwehism."

Hunger Project—Outreach of est.

"I AM" Movement—Jesus one of many ascended masters.

"I DO" Movement—Awaiting a new Savior.

Iglesia Ni Cristo—Jesus a great Savior, but not true God.

Inner Light Foundation—Meditation and spirit-guides.

Inner Peace Movement—Jesus a man who reached "Christ-consciousness"; God is impersonal.

Inner Technologies—New Age views.

Inner Vision—Mystical/astrology.

Inner Way—Mystical.

Insight Transformational Seminars—See "Church of the Movement of Spiritual Inner Awareness."

Institute for Bio-Spiritual Research—New Age views.

Institute for Family and Human Relations—Similar to "Life Training."

Institute of Divine Metaphysical Research—New Age/occult; rejects Trinity.

Institute of Mentalphysics—New Age/self-realization.

Institute of Noetic Science—Healing by mind power.

International Association of Scientologists—See "Scientology."

International Community of Christ (The Jamilians)—Christ came again in the form of Jamil Savoy (born 1959, died 1962); Christ a "universal force" to be experienced but not worshiped.

International Metaphysical Association—Similar to Christian Science.

International Society of Krishna Consciousness (ISKCON)—See "Hare Krishna."

Intuitive Explorations—New Age/magic.

Inward Bound—New Age, "universal consciousness."

Islam—Jesus a prophet of Allah who was superceded by Muhammed.

Isthmus Institute—New Age/past-life experiences.

Jamilian University of the Ordained (Jamilians)—See "International Community of Christ." Jamil was second coming of Christ.

Jainism—Deny existence of Creator; nontheistic humanists.

Jehovah's Witnesses (The Watch Tower Bible and Tract Society)—Jesus created as Archangel Michael/lesser god; became only a good man, died, ceased to exist, re-created as Michael again in heaven; not God; deny Trinity.

John-David Learning Institute—New Age views.

Joy of Living—New Age views.

Kabalarians—Speak of "Christ principle" born within every individual. See "Cabala."

Kerista Consciousness Church—New Age/goddess.

Knights of the Black Circle—Occult.

Krishnamurti Foundation of America—Disciples worship him as incarnation of God without his approval.

Laodicean Home Missionary—Splinter of Jehovah's Witnesses; deny deity of Christ.

Laughing Dove—New Age.

Latter-day Saints—See "Church of Jesus Christ of Latter-day Saints—Mormons."

Laymen's Home Missionary Movement—Christ is not God.

Lemurian Fellowship—Esoteric view of Christ.

Life Training—New Age seminars.

Life Understanding Foundation—New Age/Yoga.

Lifespring—Similar to est.

Light of Truth Church—Occult/pagan.

Lively Stones Fellowship—New Age.

Living Waters—Trinity is Father, Mother (Holy Spirit), and Son.

Love Family—See "Church of Armageddon."

Lumin Essence Productions—New Age/ascended masters.

Maharishi Ayur-Ved Foundation—Promotes Maharishi Mahesh Yogi.

Mahikari—Both Jesus and Buddha are regarded as refined spiritual beings able to radiate true light in their day.

Manifested Sons of God—Deny Trinity.

Mark-Age—New Age; believes in Christ consciousness.

Matagiri Sri Aurobindo Center Inc.—New Age/Yoga.

Mayan Order—New Age/cosmic universal force.

Megiddo Mission—Jesus wholly human in His nature.

Messianic Assemblies of Yahweh—See "Yahwehism."

Metaphysical Institute for Research and Development—New Age/Christ-consciousness.

Metaphysical Union—New Age/mystical.

The Mind Sciences—God is a principle.

Moonies—See "Unification Church."

Mormons—See "Church of Jesus Christ of Latter-day Saints."

Movement of Spiritual Inner Awareness—New Age.

Muktananda Paramahansa (Shree Gurudev Siddha Yoga Ashram)—Each person strives for his own "God-realization."

Narconon—Promotes Scientology.

Nation of Yahweh—God is black.

National Spiritual Science Center—God is all.

National Spiritualist Association of Churches—Occult.

Neo-Gnosticism—Jesus one who possessed a "higher consciousness"; did not die for man's sins.

New Age Movement—Promises to produce "Messiah" out of a coalition of cult/occult groups; usually has followers strive for "Christ-consciousness."

New Church—See "Swedenborg Foundation."

New World Publishing—New Age/pyramidology.

Nichiren Shoshu Soka Gakkai—True God replaced by Gautama Buddha and Nichiren; Bible replaced.

Niscience—New Age/meditation.

Oasis Fellowship—Similar to Unity.

Omega Institute for Holistic Studies—New Age/mystical.

Ontologists—See "Emissaries of Divine Light."

Ordo Templi Ashtart (Oto)—Splinter of Rosicrucians.

Pacific Institute—New Age/seminars.

Pastoral Bible Institute—Splinter of Jehovah's Witnesses; deny deity of Christ.

Peace Mission Movement—Sometimes states that Jesus is God, but leader George Baker has also claimed to be God and Holy Spirit.

Penitentes (Brother of Our Father Jesus)—Atonement comes by personal bloodshed rather than Christ's death and suffering.

People House—New Age.

The Peoples Temple Christian Church—Jim Jones considered himself the reincarnation of Jesus Christ and led over 900 followers to their deaths.

Philosophical Publishing Co.—See "Rosicrucians."

The Process Church of the Final Judgement—Jesus a man; three great gods are Jehovah, Lucifer, and Satan.

Proclus Society—Occult/Rosicrucianism.

Project X—See "Jamilian University."

Psychiana—Jesus a human life acting out the God-power.

Psynetic Foundation—New Age/astrology.

Quartus Foundation—New Age/metaphysical.

Radha Soami Society—Jesus one of many lords.

Radiant School—New Age/ascended masters.

Rajneesh Meditation Centers (Orange People)—God is not a person; existence is without cause.

Rastafarianisum—Mixture of African, voodooism, anamism, and Christianity.

Reiki—Buddhist healing method they claim Jesus used.

Religious Science—Similar to Christian Science.

Reorganized Church of Jesus Christ of Latter-day Saints (RLDS)—Jesus Christ existed with God in the beginning, sharing in creation.

Rev. Ike (Frederick Eikerenkoetter)—Deity is "the presence of God in you," there are no literal, spiritual realities.

Rocky Mountain Research Institute—Paranormal research.

Rosicrucianism (Rosicrucians; AMORC)—Reincarnated man is a manifestation of the cosmic Christ.

Ruhani Satsang—Jesus Christ is essentially a man of the East.

Saint Germain Foundation—Similar to "I AM" movement.

Sanatana Dharma Foundation—Jesus is a man who achieved a divine state through meditation.

Santeria—Voodoo/polytheism.

Sathya Sai Baba—Claims to be Christ and has achieved "God-realization."

School for Esoteric Studies—Jesus one of "masters of wisdom"; similar to Arcane.

Science of Mind Church—New Age views.

Scientology—All are gods, including Christ; each follower strives to become a "Thetan" (a god) by getting rid of "engrams" (past traumas).

Scripture Research Association—Believes "Jesus" and "Christ" are pagan names.

Self-Realization Church of Absolute Monism—God is all and man is God.

Shafenberg Research Foundation—New Age/occult.

Self-Realization Fellowship—Separates Jesus and Christ; Jesus was indwelt by "Christ-consciousness."

Seventh-day Adventism—Believes Jesus is God but also that he is Michael; Christ did not complete atonement at Calvary.

Sikhism—If a person works his way to salvation he is absorbed into the formless God.

Silva Mind Control—Seeks oneness with pantheistic deity; speaks of "Christ awareness."

Societas Rosicruciana in America—See "Rosicrucians."

Society of Pragmatic Mysticism—Esoteric/reincarnation.

Spiritual Advancement of the Individual Foundation—Their leader, Sai Baba, is Jesus Christ who was returned; man forgets he is God.

Spiritual Frontiers Fellowship—Jesus the man died but Christ lived; uses seances.

Spiritual Hierarchy Information Center—New Age.

Spiritual Horizons Church—Esoteric.

Spiritual Research Society—New Age views.

Spiritualists—Jesus was a Jewish medium.

Sri Chinmoy Centers—God is seen as consciousness and light. Divinity is within.

Star Center for the Americas—New Age/meditation.

Stelle Group—Followers become "one with God."

Sterling Management—Promotes Scientology.

Still Point Institute—Christ is an evolutive god, a cosmic Christ.

Subud (Gurdjieff; Renaissance Fellowship of Friends)—God is a "great life force" flowing through everything and is felt by inner vibrations; impersonal.

Sufism—God consciousness by whirling dancing.

Sufism Reoriented Inc.—Meher Baba claimed to be Christ incarnate.

Summit Lighthouse (Summit International)—See "Church Universal and Triumphant."

Summum—New Age/mummification.

Swami Kriyananda—Followers seek God-realization; Hinduistic.

Swami Rami (Himalayan International Institute of Yoga Science and Philosophy)—Combines Indian religious philosophy with psychological therapeutic techniques.

Swami Vivekananda (Vedanta Society)—Mystical Hinduism; Ramakrishna worthy of same devotion as Christ.

Swedenborgism (Swedenborg Foundation)—Calls Jesus God but denies the personality of the Holy Spirit; denies Trinity.

Taoism—Worships creator-principle of the Tao ("The Force"). Ignores Christ.

Tara Center—Looking for Maitreya (Jesus returned).

Temple of Danann—Pagan/occult.

Temple of Kriya Yoga—New Age/astrology.

Temple of the People—Mixture of "I AM" theology and theosophical philosophy.

Theosophy—Christ is the reincarnation of the world's soul.

The 3 Ho Foundation (Yogi Bhajan; Sikh Foundation)—God is cosmic consciousness; pantheistic.

TM (Transcendental Meditation)—Christ is a prophet; mankind can meditate into God-awareness without a mediator.

Transformational Seminars—New Age/stress management.

Trinity Foundation—New Age.

Triumph Publishing—Splinter of Worldwide Church of God.

Two by Twos—See "Cooneyites."

Unarius Academy of Science—Psychic/UFO.

Understanding Inc.—UFO/ESP.

The Unification Church (Also called The Holy Spirit Association; Holy Spirit Association for the Unification of World Christianity; the Unified Family; International One World Crusade; Interfaith Endeavor; "Moonies," etc.)—Believe Christ failed in His earthly mission leaving Rev. Moon to finish the task; many believe Moon to be the "Lord of the Second Advent."

Union Life—Salvation is to become Christ yourself.

Unitarians (Unitarian Universalist Assoc.)—Jesus extraordinarily good man only.

United Pentecostal Church—Denies Trinity.

Unitology Thought—Meditation/visualization.

Unity (Unity School of Christianity)—Jesus was a perfect man indwelt by the Christ-consciousness present in everybody.

Universal Christian Movement—All humans are God.

Universal Faithist of Kosmon—Occult.

Universal Life Church—Do anything you feel is right.

Universal Light of Christ Church—Christ-consciousness.

Universal Temple of Divine Light—All is God.

Universariun Foundation Inc.—New Age/ascended masters.

Urantia—Jesus a "Creator Son" called "Michael."

The Walk—See "Church of the Living Word."

The Watch Tower Bible and Tract Society—See "Jehovah's Witnesses."

The Way International—Jesus is not God.

White Dove International—New Age/occult.

Wise International—Promotes Scientology.

Wise Woman Center—Goddess worship.

World Community—New Age/mystical.

Worldwide Church of God—Denies Trinity; teaches God as a family; presently reviewing concept of God.

Yahwehism—Believes Yahweh sacred name of God; try to keep Old Law.

Yes Education Society—New Age/astrology.

Yoga (see other names listed below also)—A series of exercises and meditation designed to align your body to absorb the cosmic force.

> *Ananda Marga Yoga*—Jesus is considered God, but you, too, will become God.
>
> *Hatha Yoga*—Beginners' Yoga stressing physical exercises.
>
> *Integral Yoga Institute*—God has no name, no form, no place; evil is also God.
>
> *Shree Gurudev Siddha Yoga Ashram*—Believe leader is God.
>
> *Sivananda Yoga Vedenta Centers*—God (or Christ) is not a person or spirit but consciousness.
>
> *Tantric Yoga*—Achieving God-realization by sexual means.

You Seminars—New Age/stress management.

Zerubbabel Inc.—God is all.

Zoroastrianism—Does not recognize a personal God.